DAVID HARE

THE VERTICAL HOUR

DAVID HARE, who was born in Sussex in 1947, is one of Britain's most internationally performed playwrights. Thirteen of his plays have been produced at Britain's National Theatre. A trilogy about the Church, the Law, and the Labour Party—*Racing Demon*, *Murmuring Judges*, and *The Absence of War*—was presented in repertory at the Olivier Theatre in 1993. Nine of his best-known plays, including *Plenty*, *The Secret Rapture*, *Skylight*, *The Blue Room*, *Amy's View*, *The Judas Kiss*, and *Via Dolorosa*—in which he performed—have been presented on Broadway. His last play, *Stuff Happens*, portrayed the diplomatic process leading up to the invasion of Iraq.

THE VERTICAL HOUR

THE VERTICAL HOUR

A PLAY

DAVID HARE

FABER AND FABER, INC.
AN AFFILIATE OF FARRAR, STRAUS AND GIROUX
NEW YORK

FABER AND FABER, INC.
An affiliate of Farrar, Straus and Giroux
19 Union Square West, New York 10003

Copyright © 2006 by David Hare
All rights reserved
Printed in the United States of America
First edition, 2006

Library of Congress Control Number: 2006925415
ISBN-13: 978-0-86547-965-4
ISBN-10: 0-86547-965-8

Designed by Gretchen Achilles

www.fsgbooks.com

10 9 8 7 6 5 4 3 2 1

CAUTION: All rights whatsoever in this work are strictly reserved. Applications
for permission for any use whatsoever including performance rights must be
made in advance, prior to any such proposed use, to Casarotto Ramsay and
Associates Ltd, National House, 60-66 Wardour Street, London WIV 4ND.
No performance may be given unless a license has first been obtained.

FOR NICOLE, ALWAYS

We need, in love, to practice only this: letting each other go.
For holding on comes easily; we do not need to learn it.

—RAINER MARIA RILKE

THE VERTICAL HOUR

PRODUCTION HISTORY

The Vertical Hour had its world premiere on November 30, 2006, at the Music Box Theater in New York City. It was produced by Scott Rudin, Robert Fox, Neal Street Productions, Roger Berlind, Debra Black, and The Shubert Organization. Directed by Sam Mendes. Set design: Scott Pask. Costume design: Ann Roth. Lighting design: Brian MacDevitt. The cast was as follows:

OLIVER LUCAS	*Bill Nighy*
NADIA BLYE	*Julianne Moore*
DENNIS DUTTON	*Dan Bittner*
PHILIP LUCAS	*Andrew Scott*
TERRI SCHOLES	*Rutina Wesley*

ACT ONE

SCENE 1

OLIVER LUCAS, *alone. He is English, undemonstrative, casually dressed, in his late fifties.*

OLIVER I'd known for a long time I was going to have an accident. That's how it felt. The effort of concentration becomes impossible. For so many years you haven't made a mistake. Then you make one. It feels inevitable. You signal right, intending to go left. And you pay the price.

SCENE 2

NADIA BLYE *is leaning against the desk in her office. She is American, pale, poised, in her mid-thirties, her style casual. Opposite her is* DENNIS DUTTON, *in his early twenties, also American. He is unusually dressed for someone of his age, in suit and tie, with floppy hair and sneakers.*

NADIA This is not a bad essay.
DUTTON Thank you.
NADIA It's not bad.

DUTTON *waits.*

NADIA Clearly, I haven't persuaded you to my view of politics.
DUTTON I know your view.
NADIA It's competing claims, isn't it? If I had to sum it up. Competing claims. That's what it is.

DUTTON That's your view.

NADIA That's right. People want different things. The things they want can't be reconciled. Not everyone can *have* what they want. So the mediation between the groups, between the interest groups, the groups who want different things, to that process we give the name "politics."

NADIA *waits, but there's no reply.*

NADIA Ultimately, you could say, politics is about the reconciliation of the irreconcilable.

DUTTON I don't see it that way.

NADIA No.

DUTTON For me, politics is about the protection of property and of liberty.

NADIA Yes. Yes, that's what you seem to be saying in this essay.

DUTTON It *is* what I'm saying. It's about people's rights to live their own lives. It's about absolutes.

NADIA *thinks, considering how to go about this.*

NADIA Yes. Yes, but there's a problem, isn't there?

DUTTON Is there?

NADIA We know for a fact that human life by its nature tends toward unfairness.

DUTTON Do we know that?

NADIA I think we do. Inequality of birth. Talent. Inequality of circumstance. So: checks and balances have to be introduced. By human agency. The state, in any system yet proposed by man—be it communism, be it capitalism—has to intervene to balance things out. To prevent the weakest from being overwhelmed.

DUTTON I don't accept the term.

NADIA What term?

DUTTON "Capitalism."

NADIA *frowns.*

NADIA You don't accept the term?
DUTTON No.
NADIA You don't accept it?
DUTTON No.
NADIA Meaning? Meaning what?
DUTTON I don't think there's any such thing.
NADIA No such thing as capitalism?
DUTTON Correct.
NADIA Huh. Expand.
DUTTON What? What do you want me to say?
NADIA I suppose what I'm asking: So what name do you give it,
 then? The system we live under today? The system we call
 "consumer capitalism," "liberal democracy"—characterized by
 political parties and—I don't know—huge corporations,
 massively powerful industrial and military interests? The system
 as evolved in the West, by Western democracies? What do you
 call it?
DUTTON Life. I call it "life."

NADIA *nods slightly.*

NADIA No offense, but do you think Political Studies was a good
 choice of subject for you?
DUTTON My father wanted me to do it.
NADIA He's important to you?
DUTTON Very much so. I admire him more than anyone in the
 world.

NADIA *looks a moment, thoughtful.*

NADIA It's just . . . how do I put this? I don't know . . . basic to
 Political Studies is the notion of comparison.
DUTTON Sure.

NADIA We compare.

DUTTON Sure.

NADIA That's what we do. That's what our study is. The approach
is to say: "This is one way of looking at things. Now here's
another."

DUTTON So?

NADIA Well, to put it no higher, such comparison becomes
difficult if we start out with the idea that there's only one
system—there's only one way.

DUTTON But there is.

NADIA Is there?

DUTTON *smiles.*

DUTTON I know it's inconvenient to ask, but why do you think
America has triumphed?

NADIA *is slightly thrown.*

NADIA Inconvenient? Is "inconvenient" the word for America's
triumph? And I'm not sure I'm going to go with "triumph"
either.

DUTTON Why not? Why not "triumph"?

NADIA Listen. Listen. This is a school. It's not a madrasa.
We're not teaching one path. We're teaching many paths.
You say you admire liberal democracy. Well, basic to liberal
democracy is the idea of free discussion. The free exchange
of ideas. *Comparison.*

DUTTON You telling me I'm wrong to love America?

NADIA I'm not.

DUTTON I'm wrong to love my country?

NADIA No. I'm not telling you any such thing. I'm telling
you not to be blinded by love, that's all. Not to be made stupid
by love.

DUTTON Stupid?

There is a silence. NADIA, *embarrassed, picks up his essay and walks to the other side of the room.* DUTTON *is very quiet.*

DUTTON The fact is—I haven't wanted to say—I've come here to say this today—it's you I'm in love with.

NADIA It's me?

DUTTON I don't eat. I don't sleep. Ever since we met. Ever since—you must have noticed.

NADIA What, that—

DUTTON I've lost weight alarmingly. Have you noticed?

NADIA I haven't.

DUTTON I'm sick. I went to a barbecue on the weekend. Even the smell repelled me.

NADIA *is lost for a response.*

DUTTON I think of you all the time. I find the idea of you incredibly exciting. Of who you are.

NADIA Who I am? Say. If you imagine . . . For goodness' sake. Let's be serious! Tell me. Who am I?

DUTTON This woman out there in the world.

NADIA What woman?

DUTTON On television.

DUTTON *immediately holds up a hand.*

DUTTON All right, that was a foolish thing to say.

NADIA A tad.

DUTTON All right!

NADIA After all, there are more than a few women on television . . .

DUTTON It's not what I meant . . .

NADIA You have feelings for me because I've been on television?

DUTTON A woman in the world. That's what I mean. A woman in the world.

After the shock, NADIA *is now angry.*

NADIA Dennis, Dennis, I have to tell you, there are now quite a lot of women in the world. As you put it. Quite a lot. This isn't the 1950s. In fact, the whole assumption makes me angry. How old are you?

DUTTON Twenty-two.

NADIA I'm a feminist and what you're saying makes me angry.

DUTTON Why?

NADIA Because the purpose of women taking part, the purpose of women being intelligent or public or in any way *represented* even, the purpose of women talking on television about international politics is not to turn men on!

There is a silence. DUTTON *is very quiet.*

DUTTON You didn't know? You had no idea?

NADIA *looks, deciding how to deal with him.*

NADIA Anyway, mercifully there's a code . . .

DUTTON I know that code.

NADIA There's a code to cover this sort of ridiculous situation.

DUTTON I've actually got a copy here. I think you'll find . . .

NADIA It's not necessary. Really. Jesus!

DUTTON *has taken the code out, but* NADIA *stops him from opening it.*

NADIA So. So, one way or another, this is our last class together . . .

DUTTON Why do you think I spoke?

NADIA I'm going to ignore what you said. I'm going to forget it.

There is a brief silence.

DUTTON Can I say something?

NADIA If it's about politics, yes.

DUTTON It's all nonsense, isn't it?

NADIA I don't know what's nonsense. You tell me.

DUTTON The study of international relations.

NADIA In what way is it nonsense, Dennis?

DUTTON I took this course—as you know, I'm a business major, my interest is start-up—but my father wanted me to broaden my mind. I don't know why. Dad's own mind is about as narrow as it's possible to be.

NADIA Narrow, how?

DUTTON He wants money. That's the only thing he wants.

NADIA Well?

DUTTON *sits forward.*

DUTTON This is my point: America wins. It always wins. You can do all that historical perspective stuff, you can say it's an empire, and like any empire it's going to fall. But not yet it isn't. Not in my lifetime. So. Say there's a runner—the runner wins the race—then the other runners, if they're at all intelligent, they ask, "How did he do that?" They look at the winner, they look at his methods, they analyze, they say "Okay." And that's the way other countries are going to prosper. They'll prosper by imitating America. And to me that's Political Studies. "What does America do? And how can anyone else get close?"

NADIA Well, I'm glad my year of teaching hasn't been entirely wasted.

DUTTON It hasn't been wasted.

NADIA Good.

DUTTON In fact . . .

NADIA Dennis . . .

DUTTON That's what I wanted to say. I didn't want you to think I took this course—well, for any other reason but in order to learn. The last thing I want is to upset you.

NADIA Thank you.

DUTTON You're a brilliant teacher.

NADIA *looks wary, fearing what comes next.*

DUTTON However, we can't—face it—the other thing happened to me.

NADIA Dennis—

DUTTON It happened. I can't pretend it didn't.

NADIA I am not allowing this subject.

DUTTON I fell in love. In fact, the other day, I might as well tell you, I was talking things over with my fiancée . . .

NADIA I'm sorry? Your fiancée? *I'm sorry?*

NADIA *throws up her hands, exasperated.*

NADIA Dennis, I thought we agreed. This isn't the 1950s.

DUTTON Look, just so you understand . . .

NADIA I don't have to understand. In fact, I don't want to understand.

Now it is DUTTON*'s turn to get up, agitated.*

DUTTON It's not—it's hard—listen! *listen!*—I don't know if you don't—if you don't know Maine—anyway, two big families. In our part of the state. Big families. Both—whatever. And for many years, it's been assumed, if you like. Everyone takes it for granted. I will end up with Val. Understand.

NADIA I just said: I don't want to understand.

DUTTON But just so you know. So you know the context. Let me say: Val is not just my fiancée, she's also a friend. Val is my best friend.

NADIA And Val has no problem juggling these two roles?

DUTTON Val—talking to Val is like talking to someone—someone
objective. And it was Val who said, she said, "Look, Dennis,
you're suffering. You have been suffering. For a long time. For
your own sake, you must speak to her." It was she who suggested
it. Not me.

NADIA *looks at* DUTTON, *trying to work him out. Then she goes and sits
on the far side of the room, as if defeated.*

DUTTON I wouldn't be saying this. I wouldn't be saying it if it
were up to me.

There is a silence. When NADIA *answers she is hesitant.*

DUTTON What are you thinking?

NADIA I suppose one imagines—I imagine—the world moves
forward. Slowly, the world moves forward. My assumption has
always been that society would progress. I work on that
assumption. Old attitudes die out. But what can you say? They
don't. They don't.

DUTTON I'm not sure I understand you.

NADIA As you know, I spend a lot of time in Bosnia, in Serbia. In
many ways I can only say I prefer it there. I prefer being there
because here people—

NADIA *changes tack, not finishing her thought.*

NADIA Put it another way: I am so far from regarding myself as
somebody available to a twenty-two-year-old as simply not to
recognize myself in the description.

DUTTON But that's good, isn't it? Isn't that a good thing?

NADIA Let's say the confidence, the sheer confidence of the
moneyed class, the peculiar self-confidence based only on
accumulation, on years of accumulation, does not do it for me.

There is a silence.

NADIA This has been a profoundly depressing few minutes.

DUTTON *looks at her a moment.*

DUTTON I hear you.
NADIA Good.
DUTTON But nothing you say convinces me. As it happens, before
    I took politics, I took psychology . . .
NADIA Oh Christ!
DUTTON Briefly. Freud.
NADIA How many weeks? How many weeks did you study
    Freud?
DUTTON Three. Intensely.
NADIA Sure.
DUTTON Actually you can understand quite a lot in three weeks.
NADIA You can also misunderstand quite a lot in three weeks.
DUTTON Do you know this?
NADIA Try me.
DUTTON Freud has a theory that we aren't who we claim to be.
NADIA Really?
DUTTON Freud says we're all somebody else. Underneath.
    Underneath.
NADIA I would have thought that was self-evident. I would have
    thought that was obvious.
DUTTON Maybe it is obvious, but have you considered what it means?
NADIA Clearly, you're going to tell me I haven't.

DUTTON *leans forward, intent.*

DUTTON Think: The real person—the person concealed—is quite
    different, has quite different feelings from the person on the
    surface. Our real identity—our inner identity—bears no relation
    to the person we present to the world.

DAVID HARE

NADIA Well, it's a highly convenient theory. But that's all it is. A theory.

DUTTON So what I'm getting at is this: you don't convince me. And something tells me—my own instincts tell me—that underneath you don't even convince yourself.

NADIA *tries not to be angry.*

DUTTON I think this has happened before. I'm not the first student, am I? I know. I know you won't tell me. But I'm guessing it happens all the time. I don't see how it can't. It must. And yet for some reason you pretend it doesn't. You pretend ignorance of something you know quite a lot about.

NADIA *just looks at him.*

DUTTON I've got a feeling that's part of your attraction.

This is the last straw for NADIA. *She goes to open the door for him to leave.*

NADIA That's it. That's the end of the course. Here. Here is your essay. And the lesson's over.

DUTTON Is that it? Are we finished?

NADIA We're finished.

DUTTON Thank you very much.

NADIA No. Thank *you.*

NADIA *has given him the essay at the door, and now they have shaken hands.*

NADIA I believe I began by saying politics is about irreconcilable differences. It's about how do you reconcile people who have sharply differing views and needs? So, by that standard, we've just had a terrific political discussion.

DUTTON Yes.

DUTTON *waits a moment.*

DUTTON What are my chances of seeing you again?
NADIA They're zero.

DUTTON *nods, accepting.*

NADIA Up until now I would have dismissed you as a sort of
throwback, Dennis.
DUTTON Would you?
NADIA In all sorts of ways.
DUTTON I don't see why.
NADIA You're going into the world of money, is that right? The
world of finance.
DUTTON I'm going into my father's business.
NADIA Maybe it's my ignorance, but I don't believe that world will
be different from any other. The most important thing you can
take into it is an open mind.

DUTTON *looks at her a moment.*

DUTTON Why? Why would I want an open mind?
NADIA Why would you not?
DUTTON Our enemies don't have open minds.

SCENE 3

A lawn overlooking the Welsh and English countryside. A tree. A blissful, sunny day. There are canvas chairs. The remains of breakfast. Both OLIVER *and* PHILIP *are English, in shirtsleeves.* PHILIP LUCAS *is in his early thirties, notably handsome.*

OLIVER So tell me, tell me a little, so I know something about her before we meet.

PHILIP Aside from beautiful and brilliant?

OLIVER Aside from that, yes.

PHILIP *smiles, thinking of her.*

PHILIP Well, the first time I met her she was carrying a book: *Pas de psychologie, pas de psychose.*

OLIVER What did that mean?

PHILIP No psychology, no psychosis.

OLIVER No, I know what it means. I know what it means. I'm not an idiot. Choosing that book.

PHILIP All right, Dad.

OLIVER That's what I'm asking. What did that mean?

PHILIP *thinks a moment.*

PHILIP Well. As you know, Nadia teaches at Yale . . .

OLIVER I know that . . .

PHILIP Obviously what she was trying to say is that she isn't keen on the psychological.

OLIVER I see.

PHILIP She has a horror of it. I thought, That's refreshing. That's a refreshing approach.

OLIVER Why? Why did you think that?

PHILIP Oh. Because the first thing you notice, it becomes a way of
     life. People are taught to say, "I think, I feel." They talk all the
     time as if there were no such thing as reality.

OLIVER Really?

PHILIP Or rather: they know reality exists, they know it's there,
     but they can't help believing that what they feel about it is
     somehow more important.

OLIVER You're talking about Americans?

PHILIP Not only. But obviously. Having spent time there.

OLIVER You've noticed?

PHILIP At work. Maybe you report an event. Say: "People were
     dying," you say. And the first response is: "Really? They were
     dying? How did that make you feel?"

OLIVER That's funny.

PHILIP Yeah, but it's decadent, isn't it? As if it's not the world, it's
     not the world you're interested in, it's just your own reaction.

OLIVER *looks at him a moment.*

OLIVER Huh.

PHILIP I'll give you an example. If you take the former
     Yugoslavia . . .

OLIVER Yes?

PHILIP Nadia told me when she first went out there, she said to
     someone, "I think this is really important." Whereupon the
     person looked at her and said, "Have you noticed, you seem
     quite emotional, Nadia? Have you ever stopped and asked
     yourself *why*? All this fascination with foreign trouble spots,
     have you ever considered there might be a reason? Has it
     occurred to you, you may just be running away from problems
     in your own life?"

PHILIP *smiles at the absurdity of the question.*

DAVID HARE

OLIVER Well?

PHILIP Well, what?

OLIVER How did Nadia reply? *Did* Nadia have problems?

PHILIP I don't think so. Not that she's told me about.

They both smile.

PHILIP No, on the contrary. Nadia replied, "I'm not going to Yugoslavia because there's anything wrong with me. I'm going because there's something wrong in Yugoslavia. It's called ethnic cleansing. And it exists."

PHILIP *laughs.*

PHILIP It's crazy. It's ridiculous, isn't it?

OLIVER To be honest, I can't imagine.

PHILIP Why not?

OLIVER Because the people who need me so obviously need me.

NADIA *comes out onto the lawn.*

PHILIP Ah, there you are.

OLIVER Good morning.

NADIA *reaches out a hand.*

NADIA Hello.

OLIVER Oliver.

NADIA I'm sorry. I overslept.

PHILIP It's fine. Everyone's fine.

NADIA So.

The three of them stand a moment, embarrassed.

PHILIP Well . . .

OLIVER Let me—right—to give you the idea, has anyone explained?

NADIA No.

OLIVER This is border country. That way, the sea. That way, the south.

NADIA Toward the sun.

OLIVER Precisely.

NADIA Goodness, I really did oversleep.

PHILIP It's not like you.

NADIA It isn't.

PHILIP You always wake up so early.

OLIVER You drove through the night, so I don't know how much you saw. Philip said you'd only been to England once before.

PHILIP For a conference.

NADIA At Chatham House. International relations. It was brief.

OLIVER *looks at her a moment.*

OLIVER Excuse me one moment. At least I'm going to make you a cup of coffee.

OLIVER *goes out.*

NADIA Hell I'm nervous. I didn't expect to be nervous. I'm not used to this. I'm usually in charge.

PHILIP Why be nervous? You had to meet him sometime.

NADIA Sure. Just remind me, why did I have to meet him?

PHILIP You need to meet them both?

NADIA You're not nervous?

PHILIP *just smiles.*

NADIA I love your calm. I wish I had your calm. Not just today. Always.

PHILIP *kisses her.*

PHILIP Good morning.
NADIA Any chance I can borrow it?

OLIVER *is already returning.*

OLIVER Philip's tried to tell me what you do. I can't say I
understand it entirely.
NADIA I'm not sure I do either.
PHILIP Did you put the coffee on?
OLIVER Yes. Fresh.
PHILIP I'll get you something to eat.
NADIA Oh . . .
PHILIP No, really.
OLIVER Do you need my help?
PHILIP No. I know where everything is.

PHILIP *goes out, smiling to himself.*

OLIVER So tell me. Please. I wouldn't ask if I didn't want to know.
NADIA Very well, then.
OLIVER Thank you.
NADIA At its simplest: Arrive from Mars, first thing you'd notice,
one-tenth of the planet doing well, nine-tenths less well.
OLIVER That's where you start?
NADIA It's the given, isn't it? It's a fact. Come from Mars, that's
how it looks. I remember, very early on, when I was in tenth
grade, thinking: Half the world lives on less than two dollars a
day, 1.3 billion have no access to clean water, 2 billion no access
to electricity, 3 billion no access to sanitation. And thinking:
Why doesn't everyone talk about this all the time?
OLIVER Tenth grade? That's . . .
NADIA Around fifteen.
OLIVER Ah yes.

NADIA But it seemed so shocking. So much time in the classroom spent reading—I don't know—medieval literature, doing trigonometry, and all the time—

OLIVER Yes.

NADIA These huge facts, these enormous facts not up for study. Ignored.

OLIVER *looks at her, thoughtful.*

NADIA Of course, now, so many years later, I admit, my work touches less directly on these disparities. Or only obliquely.

OLIVER But the impulse?

NADIA Yes.

NADIA *smiles.*

NADIA And I'm mystified by why so few people are interested.

OLIVER Quite.

NADIA You'd think that to be alive would mean to want to find out. Why so many people live in such poverty. And so few live well. And what can we do about it?

OLIVER *looks at her a moment.*

OLIVER But specifically . . .

NADIA Yes?

OLIVER Philip had suggested . . .

NADIA Yes?

OLIVER Your area is now international relations?

NADIA That's right.

OLIVER Your specific concern.

NADIA My field.

OLIVER With a particular interest in terror.

NADIA Oh no, not "particular."

OLIVER Philip says you're known as the professor of terror.

NADIA Well, occasionally, only in the media. And among a few of my students. The dumber ones.

OLIVER Do you have stupid students?

NADIA I'm afraid I do. Or at least I was thinking before I left.

OLIVER Why? Why before you left?

NADIA Oh, something that happened. A student. My God. Made me think.

NADIA *smiles.*

OLIVER But you have written about terror?

NADIA Of course. Everyone does. You can't do what I do and not be fascinated by it.

OLIVER *waits for her to go on.*

NADIA All right, crudely, if you're asking, you can say, if you want to put it this way, that terrorism may be the wrong answer to the right question.

OLIVER What question is that?

NADIA Well, I'd have thought terror's an attack on modernity, isn't it?

OLIVER Is it?

NADIA Isn't it, in some part, an attack on the modern world, on what certain people feel the world has become?

OLIVER I'm never sure. Tell me what "modernity" means.

NADIA Usually it means that human beings feel themselves discontent, they feel lost in the world—if there's nothing *but* the world—and they imagine that materialism must therefore be at fault.

NADIA *shifts.*

NADIA Of course—look, not to insult you—it's much more complicated than that . . .

OLIVER Of course . . .

NADIA And the actual *motivation* . . .

OLIVER Yes . . .

NADIA . . . the moment at which an individual picks up a gun, or
prepares explosives—that moment is still deeply obscure. People
claim to understand it, but do they? I certainly don't. But
underlying that desire you'll often find the same discontent:
namely, the conviction that materialism isn't enough.

OLIVER And is that what you think?

NADIA People who blame materialism blame it because they feel it
doesn't nourish them. And you could say it's true: materialism,
by definition, isn't heroic. In the West we no longer prize
heroism. People no longer want to do dangerous, outstanding
things. All they want is to live as long and as comfortably as
possible. And so this new Western ethic of survival, simply
surviving as a human being—merely surviving—as though the
world were everything, and the manner in which you live in it
secondary—seems to other people, other cultures . . . well,
ignoble.

OLIVER Do you agree?

NADIA Me?

OLIVER Is that your own view? Do you feel that?

NADIA *looks at him a moment.*

NADIA I don't know. But, whether it is or not, the answer isn't
violence.

PHILIP *appears on the lawn.*

PHILIP I'm assuming you want toast.

NADIA Yes, please.

PHILIP Honey or jam?

NADIA Honey. No, jam. Honey.

PHILIP I'll bring both.

PHILIP *goes.* NADIA *remembers after he's gone.*

NADIA Thanks, babe!

OLIVER In fact, out of curiosity I admit I did go to your
website . . .

NADIA Oh, that . . .

OLIVER It lists subjects about which you're available
to speak.

NADIA It's a fancy piece of publicity. Shaming, but you have to
do it.

OLIVER Do you?

NADIA Sure.

OLIVER Why's that?

NADIA Being an academic isn't quite what it was. We find
ourselves doing all sorts of things.

OLIVER I see.

NADIA Inevitably, yes, I talk to the media.

OLIVER You make a point of it?

NADIA *looks a moment, detecting criticism.*

NADIA I was mentioning earlier about privilege? And my special
privilege has been to define my job as I go along.

OLIVER You're free?

NADIA That's it.

OLIVER Free to do what you choose?

NADIA More or less. The university's been very generous.

OLIVER Because of your status?

NADIA If you choose to put it like that. I barely teach. A couple of
seminars. Mostly, I write.

OLIVER Philip said.

NADIA One book already. Another on the way. This is a relatively
new study. Or rather it's an old study which has been
transformed. Am I boring you?

OLIVER No.

NADIA You'll let me know if I'm boring you.

OLIVER You're not.

NADIA As long as we had two great powers, two superpowers in some sort of balance, then there seemed to be a procedure—however inadequate, however faulty—for determining the world's affairs.

OLIVER Now there's only one.

NADIA Exactly. So because of this imbalance—one powerful country, others powerless—questions of international justice become far more complex. My area of study becomes more vital.

OLIVER Especially after Iraq.

NADIA As you say. Yes. Especially after Iraq.

NADIA looks again, trying to gauge his agenda. Then she gets up and moves to look out over the hills.

NADIA I didn't get much of a look last night, but this wasn't what I was expecting.

OLIVER This spot?

NADIA Yes.

OLIVER In what way?

NADIA I knew you were alone. But even so.

OLIVER I am alone.

NADIA Is that a choice?

OLIVER Well, this place wouldn't be chance, would it?

NADIA How do you pronounce it?

OLIVER Shrewsbury.

They smile together.

OLIVER I came here over ten years ago.

NADIA As long as that? And you don't mind? You don't mind the isolation?

OLIVER Philip was already practicing. He'd gone, he'd left home.

NADIA His mother brought him up?

OLIVER Officially, yes. But I did my share. You haven't met her yet?

NADIA No. No, I haven't. He wants me to.

OLIVER *gestures around.*

OLIVER There aren't many spots left where you can turn 360 degrees and see barely a single building.

NADIA You went out of your way?

OLIVER In France they have this expression: *France profonde.*

NADIA I'm embarrassed. I don't speak French.

OLIVER No? I'm surprised.

NADIA Why? Why does that surprise you?

OLIVER Oh, something Philip said.

NADIA What was that?

OLIVER *is reluctant.*

NADIA No, say.

OLIVER *Pas de psychologie. Pas de psychose.*

There is a moment. NADIA *seems displeased.*

NADIA He told you that? Why did he tell you that?

OLIVER I'm sorry, have I crossed some sort of line?

NADIA No, no, no.

OLIVER Please, I didn't mean to upset you.

NADIA You haven't upset me.

OLIVER I happened to ask him how you met, that's all.

NADIA *turns away.*

NADIA It's silly. Why do I want private things to be private?

PHILIP *returns with coffee and toast for* NADIA.

PHILIP You two all right?
NADIA We are. Thank you.
OLIVER Fine.

NADIA *takes her breakfast from him.*

NADIA Obviously you and your dad were talking while I was
  asleep.
PHILIP Oh, not much.
OLIVER No.
PHILIP Very little, in fact.
OLIVER Philip's one of those people who's always been at peace
  with silence.
PHILIP Silence never bothered me.
OLIVER If the world can be divided into those who need to speak
  and those who don't.
PHILIP People only talk because they're nervous.
OLIVER It's funny. There's a doctor at the hospital who's notorious
  for his pauses. Ear, Nose, and Throat. "What are my chances,
  Doctor?" "Well . . ."

OLIVER *pauses elaborately.*

OLIVER If the patient doesn't die of the disease, they die of
  anxiety.
NADIA And you?
OLIVER Me?
NADIA How's your manner?
OLIVER Oh, reasonably sympathetic, I hope. Early on, they taught
  me something I try not to forget.
NADIA What's that?
OLIVER The definition of a doctor.
NADIA I've never heard it. Tell me.

OLIVER A doctor is someone who tells you the truth and stays
with you to the end.

NADIA *stops eating and looks directly at him.*

OLIVER Not bad, eh?
NADIA No. Not bad.
OLIVER It's pretty good, isn't it?

PHILIP *shifts, not sure what's going on.*

PHILIP Are we going into town? I'd like to show Nadia the town.

OLIVER *takes no notice.*

OLIVER Nadia's been explaining how things have changed for the
academic. The public role.
NADIA Your father sounds as if he disapproves.
OLIVER Not at all.
NADIA As if it were vulgar.
OLIVER Not vulgar, no. I have my own idea of what it is to be a
professional. The two requirements: to be objective and to be
discreet.
NADIA I'd hope I was both of those.

OLIVER *looks at her a moment.*

OLIVER Philip mentioned . . . Philip did mention that the
president asked for you.
NADIA He did. Believe it or not, he did.
OLIVER You went to the White House?
NADIA I did.
OLIVER Goodness.
NADIA I know.
OLIVER What did he want?

NADIA Oh, you can imagine.

OLIVER Actually, no. I have no idea.

NADIA He wanted briefing. He wanted advice.

OLIVER Which you were able to give?

NADIA *doesn't answer.*

OLIVER About Iraq?

NADIA Yes. He knew I'd written about Iraq.

OLIVER Clearly you were in favor? You were in favor of the invasion?

NADIA The liberation, yes. Yes, I was in favor. I don't think the president would have asked me if I wasn't.

OLIVER No.

They both smile.

NADIA Whatever you think, whatever your view, I'd have to say it is undeniably something.

OLIVER For you?

NADIA No, I'm not talking personally. I'm talking about entering. Walking in. It's impressive. You're picked up at your hotel in a black car, with blacked-out windows. Five minutes later you're standing on the carpet in the Oval Office.

OLIVER It's theater?

NADIA That's right. Theater.

NADIA *looks down, slightly embarrassed.*

NADIA Also, in our country, it isn't just the person, it's the office.

OLIVER He's the president.

NADIA In America . . . in America that still means something.

OLIVER Quite.

NADIA It really does. Do I sound naive?

OLIVER I don't think so.

NADIA Because from what people tell me, it's not the same here.

OLIVER Not in the smallest degree.

NADIA Why is that?

OLIVER It's hard to explain. But I'm probably typical.

PHILIP Dad is absolutely typical.

NADIA How?

PHILIP *smiles, dodging the question.*

PHILIP I left this country, remember?

OLIVER No doubt you feel that if your president calls, you have to
answer that call. If my prime minister called, I'd let it ring. That's
the difference.

PHILIP It's true.

OLIVER And what's more, *what's more,* politics being what it is in
this country—i.e., everything, *everything*—my prime minister
wouldn't call me in the first place.

PHILIP That's definitely true.

NADIA Do you—I don't know how to ask this—am I ridiculous
for asking this?

OLIVER Ask.

NADIA Does no one here have any concept of national loyalty? Of
being part of a nation?

OLIVER Oh.

NADIA Well?

OLIVER I don't know how to answer. Like most people, I do have
a button marked "patriotism." But—let's say—I'm choosy about
who I allow to press it. Certainly not politicians. And certainly
not the Queen.

NADIA Who, then?

OLIVER Oh, you know. Poets. Blake. Wilfred Owen.

There's a silence. Nobody moves.

OLIVER An appeal to patriotism is a contradiction in terms.
Especially when made by politicians. You can no more appeal to
patriotism than you can appeal to love. You may feel it, but you
can't demand it. Wilfred Owen, yes. Fifty-seven thousand British
casualties on the first morning on the battle of the Somme, sent
into a murderous war by the ruthless, out-of-touch political class
of the day. Men with no direct experience of war, and no
knowledge of its reality, send ordinary workingmen to fight on
their behalf. Hello? Hard to explain, impossible to justify. And
one man—one great man—adequate to describe the event.

PHILIP *smiles to himself.*

PHILIP Dad liked the Sex Pistols as well.
OLIVER I admit it.
PHILIP Same reason.
OLIVER Similar.
PHILIP All right . . .
OLIVER Not the same.
PHILIP Okay.
OLIVER Don't make me sound stupid. But I did like the Sex Pistols.

OLIVER *sits back, expansive.*

OLIVER The only patriotic outfit still operating in this country is
the awkward squad. In the United States, you're building an
empire. Remember, we've dismantled one. When Philip was
young I remember him saying he'd like to be gay or an
immigrant because then he'd belong. He wanted a tribe.
NADIA Isn't medicine a tribe?
OLIVER Used to be. Now it's freelance. We've been—what's the
word?—outsourced. The politicians dismantle communities,
then complain that community no longer exists. They incubate
the disease, then profess to be shocked when people catch it.

DAVID HARE

"Oh, why can't people behave?" Well, why can't they? It's a good question. When the people who make the law become lawless themselves, what can you do? How can politicians lead except by example?

NADIA *smiles, giving up.*

NADIA You have a high standard.

OLIVER I suppose I do.

NADIA If you're talking about what I think you're talking about.

PHILIP I don't think there's much doubt, is there?

OLIVER I don't think there is.

PHILIP It's a fair chance, one way or another, Dad's returned to the subject of Iraq.

OLIVER How did you know?

NADIA Oh, I see.

PHILIP He usually does.

OLIVER "Usually"?

PHILIP All right . . .

OLIVER I don't think, Philip, you're in a position to say "usually."

PHILIP I agree. I'm not.

OLIVER "Usually" when you never see me?

PHILIP Okay . . .

OLIVER Not just don't see me, barely ever talk, don't even talk to me.

PHILIP Whose fault is that?

OLIVER I know. I'm just saying. For all that.

An edgy silence. NADIA *puts her plate aside.*

NADIA Good, well, maybe this is the moment to set off for Shrewsbury.

OLIVER Maybe it is.

They smile at one another.

NADIA Believe me, if it's what you want, I'm happy to have the Iraq discussion.

OLIVER I'm not asking for it.

NADIA I'll have it tonight if you want.

OLIVER I'm not insisting.

NADIA I've had it every day for the last three years. I never supposed a vacation in England would be a vacation from the argument.

OLIVER Quite.

NADIA Why should today be different?

NADIA *gets up and turns, formal.*

NADIA No doubt, you can imagine, I've taken a huge amount of flak.

OLIVER I'm sure.

NADIA In liberal Connecticut defending the war has not been a popular position.

OLIVER It's not been big in Shropshire either.

NADIA If you're interested: I was quite clear about why I supported it. I'm also clear about what's gone wrong. And I don't think the mess that's followed invalidates the original decision. I've always supported humane intervention in countries where terrible things are happening. I believe in it. With all my heart. If the choice is between stepping in or staying put and watching dictators let rip, not least against their own people, then I'm for stepping in. I was a reporter before I was an academic. I've been in these places. I've seen suffering—at ground level. And I've been present in situations in which the West did nothing. I've seen the results of our indifference. So. If you want me to pass my evening defending the right of Western countries to use their muscle to free Arabs from systematic murder, believe me, I'm up for it.

OLIVER I'm sure you are.

NADIA I take it you were against?

OLIVER Passionately.

NADIA From the beginning?

OLIVER Let's just say, I knew who the surgeon was going to be, so I had a fair idea what the operation would look like.

OLIVER *gets up.*

OLIVER Please. Don't take it amiss. I'm not being rude.

NADIA I know that.

OLIVER Least of all to you, to you of all people, Nadia. I'm thrilled my son has brought somebody home. Even if it isn't home. In the proper sense.

There's a moment. OLIVER *speaks quietly.*

OLIVER All I want is Philip's happiness.

NADIA We want the same thing.

OLIVER And if you can contribute to that happiness, then believe me nobody could be more welcome.

There's a brief silence.

NADIA However.

OLIVER I'm sorry?

NADIA I sense a "however."

OLIVER No. There is no "however."

They look at each other a moment.

NADIA Excuse me. I'll get my things.

She goes off into the house. PHILIP *moves away,* OLIVER *doesn't move. A few moments go by.*

PHILIP Can I just say: This is an act of trust. I trusted you!

OLIVER Well?

PHILIP Dad, I didn't have to do this. I did it because I wanted to.

OLIVER So?

There is a silence. OLIVER *says nothing.*

PHILIP It's my own fault. I have this ridiculous need for family.

OLIVER Why ridiculous?

PHILIP Apart from anything, because I'm the only person in my family who has it.

OLIVER Your mother has it.

PHILIP *throws him a mistrustful look.*

PHILIP Just look at Nadia. You see what she is! You can tell what she is! This is the best piece of luck in my life! Meeting her! What, I'm not to marry her because you don't approve of her position on Iraq?

OLIVER Come on, nobody said that.

PHILIP Didn't they?

OLIVER Nobody put it like that.

PHILIP They didn't need to, did they?

OLIVER And maybe I wasn't listening, but I didn't hear anyone say "marriage" either.

PHILIP *is silent.* OLIVER *is amused.*

OLIVER What am I meant to say? What have I done wrong?

PHILIP You know full well.

OLIVER Do I?

PHILIP You could be a little more welcoming.

OLIVER Welcoming?

PHILIP Yes.

OLIVER Come on, it's been a good old Welsh-borders welcome. What was missing? Conjuring tricks?

But PHILIP *has already moved away.*

PHILIP She said, "I'd be fascinated to see a little family
  background." It's not very easy, is it? To explain, "Oh, you can
  meet my father, but bear in mind, this is a man who destroyed
  my mother's life."

OLIVER Did I?

PHILIP And now—for reasons I'm not going into—he lives alone on
  a hillside, repelling boarders. Or rather, repelling male boarders.

OLIVER *smiles, unperturbed, enjoying himself.*

OLIVER Philip, this is a tense and unnatural situation.

PHILIP You could say.

OLIVER Of course it is. It will test both of our characters to the
  limit.

PHILIP Very funny.

OLIVER Neither of us—all right?—has too much experience of
  conventional family life.

PHILIP To put it no higher.

OLIVER But, in my opinion, I think you're letting it get to you.

OLIVER *sits back, content.*

OLIVER You say she's the greatest piece of luck in your life.

PHILIP She is.

OLIVER In that case, you might ask, why risk your luck by
  bringing her here to meet me?

PHILIP I'm beginning to ask that myself.

OLIVER Well, then, why did you?

PHILIP *just looks at him.*

OLIVER All right. In fact, take one step back and I think you'll
  find the whole thing is going remarkably well.

PHILIP You think so?

OLIVER She's enjoying my company and relishing the chance to talk to someone who's almost as clever as she is.

PHILIP You mean as opposed to me?

OLIVER *looks at him reproachfully.*

OLIVER Look, Philip, if you'd like a piece of advice . . .

PHILIP Advice from you?

OLIVER . . . then I'd say—just from my own experience—I have some experience of this—strategically it wouldn't be very clever when in Nadia's company to show self-doubt. Trust me. It would not be advantageous. Because—I admit, you know her better than I do—but my guess is that Nadia Blye is not someone who easily tolerates weakness. She doesn't *like* it. Am I right?

PHILIP *doesn't answer.*

OLIVER Anyone who announces that psychology's a load of rubbish—well, you choose to call that attitude "refreshing." I think a better word for it might be "dangerous." That's all I'm saying.

PHILIP You've said enough.

OLIVER Take one look at her: she's someone who'd have very little trouble attracting any man on campus.

PHILIP So?

OLIVER So my guess is, she's picked you out because you appear to be strong. Well, then. Be strong. Why disappoint her? As our government instructs us, be alert but not alarmed. Face it: nothing serious is going to go wrong unless you let it go wrong.

There is a mistrustful silence.

PHILIP We're leaving tomorrow. We're leaving tomorrow night.

OLIVER Good. Then we'll all take it step by step and see how it goes.

OLIVER *examines his nails, smiling.* PHILIP *is annoyed with himself.*

PHILIP And I don't feel self-doubt when I'm in America.
OLIVER Good.
PHILIP I like American life.
OLIVER I'm sure you do.
PHILIP I like the feel of it. The texture. It suits me. In America, I stand with a gin and tonic, I look out of the window, people are going out to the mall, and I feel hopeful. Explain that.
OLIVER I can't.
PHILIP The landscape moves me. Crazy, isn't it? When there's a road across the desert and nothing in sight. When it snows in New England. Sobbing like a child about a place that isn't even home.

OLIVER *looks down, mischievous.*

OLIVER Well, it's always nice, isn't it? To get away from one's parents . . . And what's more, with an American girlfriend. Though, from what I read in the magazines, American women can be quite exacting.

PHILIP *turns, half amused, half exasperated.*

PHILIP Oh God, are you off again?
OLIVER Am I?
PHILIP Why do you do this? My whole life, you did this stuff. Did nobody tell you? Kids aren't meant to be objects of satire, you know. That's not why most people opt for parenthood.
OLIVER No, you're right.
PHILIP Most people don't use their children to refine their jokes on.
OLIVER I know. Absolutely.
PHILIP Well?
OLIVER You're right. Of course you're right.
PHILIP You're fifty-eight. It's unbecoming.

OLIVER I'll stop.

NADIA *returns.*

PHILIP Ah, there you are. Good, you're ready. I'll get the car keys.
NADIA I've got them here.

NADIA *holds them out.*

NADIA Are you coming with us?
OLIVER I'm not. You enjoy yourselves.

NADIA *hesitates, about to go.*

NADIA I was thinking, something about this situation reminds me
   of J. Paul Getty. Do you know who I mean?
OLIVER Of course.
NADIA Richest man in the world. I've always liked him for one
   thing.
OLIVER What was that?
NADIA I read, before he took a girl on their first date, he insisted she
   submit to a full medical examination by a doctor of his choosing.

OLIVER *and* NADIA *smile.*

NADIA Now that's what I call romantic.
OLIVER Me too.
NADIA Great start to an evening, isn't it?
OLIVER And good business for my profession too.
NADIA Yeah. Yeah, that's what I was thinking.

The two of them stand, amused by each other.

NADIA See you later.
OLIVER And you.

SCENE 4

The lawn again. The remains of a meal. A CD player is on in the house.
NADIA, PHILIP, *and* OLIVER *have been eating at a table under the stars.*
It looks enchanting.

NADIA It seems so long ago, it seems like such a long time ago. I
  suppose I wasn't there more than eight months . . .
OLIVER That's all?
NADIA Probably. But it seems like half a lifetime. It's true: there's a
  special kind of intimacy that comes from danger.
OLIVER Perhaps.
NADIA When we were in Sarajevo.

There's a moment's silence.

NADIA Maybe there was something about my being so young.
  Most of us were. By the time you've got a family, it's tough,
  unless your partner's willing to accept you might get a bullet in
  the throat.

OLIVER *refers to the scene around them.*

OLIVER You couldn't sit under the stars? You couldn't eat out?
NADIA You couldn't eat. Most nights I was looped, all of us were.
OLIVER Looped? What does "looped" mean?

There is a sudden silence. She looks at him.

NADIA Looped? Looped means drunk.

Everyone is still, PHILIP *watching intently.*

NADIA You'd go out all day in what we call "soft skins" . . .

OLIVER Say again.

NADIA I thought it would amuse you, that's why I said it.

OLIVER All your correspondents' slang.

NADIA Yeah . . .

OLIVER You're a tribe.

NADIA Hmm.

OLIVER So, "soft skin"?

NADIA "Soft skin," meaning a car with no armor. An unarmored car. A regular car. Like that one over there.

OLIVER So you went into Shrewsbury today . . .

NADIA Yeah . . .

OLIVER In a soft skin.

NADIA That's right. Only in Sarajevo you felt it, you really felt it, because you knew there was just a thin layer of tin between you and everything outside. Back at the hotel you were sharing rooms, maybe sleeping on the floor, depending, depending for your life on each other's character, each other's intelligence. You made friends for life.

OLIVER *waits.*

OLIVER But you stopped?

NADIA Oh, yes.

OLIVER You no longer do it. Why?

NADIA The whole thing. The anger. I found myself addicted.

OLIVER Which? To the anger or the way of life?

NADIA Both.

OLIVER Anger against what?

NADIA Anger against the world. The world, for standing by, for knowing and not intervening.

NADIA *shakes her head, remembering.*

NADIA Endless days, days lying on a floor in a blackout, watching people die for no purpose, for no reason, except the world's laziness, its fat, spoiled sense of itself, its stupid fascination with handbags and losing body weight and who won the Open and who takes an iron to the green. Who cares? Who the fuck cares? The first great war in Europe since 1945 and nobody is able even to remember which country is which. Which one's Milosevic and which one's the other guy? And which is Croatia, remind me? Is that the one full of Muslims? Or is that Bosnia? I mean, who are we? Who the fuck are we?

There's a moment's silence. Is she drunk? OLIVER*'s gaze is steady.*

NADIA Three hundred thousand people killed in Europe.
OLIVER You still feel it.
NADIA Yes. I feel it. When I've had a few drinks.

NADIA *acknowledges the glass in her hand.*

NADIA Philip's heard it before.
PHILIP I don't mind.

PHILIP *smiles a little, reassuring.*

NADIA Forgive me. It's a drug. The anger's a drug. I don't like that part of myself.
OLIVER You think it's unattractive?
NADIA I don't give a fuck if it's attractive. I only care what it feels like, and it doesn't feel good.
OLIVER Because?
NADIA For the obvious reason.
OLIVER What's that?
NADIA What, I'm supposed to spend all my time believing that everyone's wrong except me? The world is uncaring and ignorant except for me? Please!
OLIVER I understand.
NADIA No, walking around feeling *that* all the time doesn't make

anyone happy—unless of course they're a psychopath, or—I don't know—one of your poets.

NADIA *stares a moment, the anger unabated.*

OLIVER And that's the reason you stopped?
NADIA I went out a reporter. I came back an analyst.
OLIVER Maybe your temperament was wrong.
NADIA Maybe.
OLIVER Psychologically.

NADIA *looks up, sharply.* OLIVER *smiles.*

OLIVER To use that word.
NADIA Look, it was simple. It was a simple thing.
OLIVER Was it?
NADIA Yes. Don't make it out to be complex. At the end of it all, when I wasn't plain scared or exhausted, I just felt, shit, I'm spending too much of my time feeling self-righteous.
OLIVER Why? Why self-righteous?
NADIA Oh, look—whatever—half self-righteous, half confused. "Oh, you're a foreign correspondent. How fascinating!" Well yes, it would be fascinating if anyone took any notice of what we said . . .
OLIVER Yes.
NADIA If anyone listened! If anyone did anything because of what we reported!

OLIVER *waits, tactful.*

OLIVER But actually you were right. You were right to be angry. Why should you be ashamed? Those people *did* die. And nobody *did* care. Why to apologize?

NADIA *looks at him a moment, thoughtful.*

NADIA There were nights so cold, so pitted from the trace of machine-gun fire, I didn't know concrete could have so many holes and still stand. Like latticework. There were bodies—every shape, every color, bodies rotting in the woods, on building sites—ceaseless, pointless violence, dinning in your head so you wanted to scream. And three hundred miles away there were people going to the opera and hailing gondolas and laughing, not wanting to know, not needing to know. Because they didn't believe the war would come anywhere near them.

OLIVER *reaches tactfully for the bottle and refills her glass.* NADIA *shakes her head.*

NADIA Well, now they have their war, and much good may it do them. It's wrong to blame them. The truth is, there was far more terrorism in the 1980s, when nobody thought about it, than there is today, when nobody thinks about anything else. It's just a fact.

NADIA *smiles, relaxing at the irony. She reaches for* PHILIP*'s hand.*

NADIA In fact, we went—didn't we?—we went to a conference . . .
OLIVER Where was this?
NADIA Helsinki.
PHILIP Helsinki was interesting.
NADIA Philip came.
PHILIP Just for fun. I was Mr. Blye.
NADIA A man got up, very early on, said, "Nobody in this room is going to die of terrorism. Let's start from there. You're more likely to die from swallowing a wasp than you are from meeting a suicide bomber."
PHILIP That's what he said.
NADIA He didn't make himself popular. Not in that company.

They both smile at the memory.

PHILIP Actually, I talked to him later in the bar.

NADIA You did. I remember.

PHILIP We had a beer. "The point of a conference," he said, "is to be the person who says the stupidest thing."

PHILIP *smiles, anticipating* NADIA.

PHILIP All right, maybe he didn't say "stupid" . . .

NADIA Ah well, no . . .

PHILIP Maybe he said "provocative." "Memorable." I don't know.

NADIA "Memorable," "stupid"—there is a difference.

PHILIP Anyway, we know what he meant. He said, "That's intellectual life in the West." He was Egyptian. "That way you make a reputation," he said. "It's a game."

NADIA *is looking disapproving.*

PHILIP It's not what I think, sweet one, it's just what he said.

NADIA *laughs, forgiving* PHILIP.

NADIA It's funny. It was a funny weekend to begin with. I made this stupid mistake . . .

PHILIP I didn't mind.

NADIA I've promised Philip I'll never do it again.

PHILIP It's just those people. They have no idea.

OLIVER Which people?

NADIA I happened to mention to someone what Philip did for a living.

PHILIP Yeah.

NADIA Well . . .

PHILIP Who'd have thought so many intellectuals had such bad backs?

NADIA And such a poor idea of how to behave. Not a single one of them didn't sneak up to Philip at some point in the weekend.

NADIA *is gathering pace, excited.*

NADIA People—can I say this—?

PHILIP Sure . . .

NADIA They have this idea of physiotherapy as if it were some kind of trade. As if it were plumbing. They treat him as if he's some kind of natural resource.

PHILIP It's ignorance.

NADIA I'd never met a physio till I met Philip, but even I knew they're not the kind of people you press sweaty bills into their hands. In fact, I tell you, there was one woman there . . .

PHILIP *rolls his eyes.*

PHILIP Oh Jesus!

NADIA Well, it's what happened . . .

PHILIP Nadia doesn't care for my female clients anyway.

NADIA I don't think that's true. I don't think that's true at all.

PHILIP Don't you?

NADIA No. As a matter of fact, I don't. And I don't know why you say it. I really don't.

PHILIP All right, let's say—how do I put this—

NADIA I don't know. How *will* you put this?

PHILIP All right. At the best of times, Nadia distrusts my female clients of a certain age, of a certain appearance . . .

NADIA Some of them aren't in quite as much pain as they pretend.

It's badinage, but it's spiked. OLIVER *observes closely.*

PHILIP Anyway, one way or another, this woman's Italian.

NADIA Attractive.

PHILIP Sort of good-looking. Full-figured.

NADIA Expert on early jihad.

PHILIP She says, "Can you possibly just pop up to my room and attend to my grinding discs?"

PHILIP *raises his voice to preempt their reaction.*

PHILIP I would like to say, can I just say, this woman is one of the
  foremost academics in Italy? One of the cleverest women in Italy.
OLIVER What did you say?
PHILIP I said, Listen, signora, as a matter of fact, you may not believe
  this, but in the United States of America I get two hundred and
  fifty dollars an hour for what I do. And I deserve it. And anyway,
  I'm on vacation, learning about the pathology of terrorism.
OLIVER What did she say? What did she say to that?
PHILIP I think she was surprised.

He grins, but NADIA *is already continuing.*

NADIA I'd already gotten the hang of this woman.
PHILIP You'd taken against her. Big-time.
NADIA Oh, forgive me, but she was one of those self-hating
  liberals.
OLIVER Oh, one of those.
NADIA "It's our fault. They're right to hate us. If I were them, I'd
  hate us, too." You know the type.
OLIVER I do.
NADIA It's dressed up. It comes all wrapped up in fancy talk, but
  underneath.

NADIA *puts up a hand to forestall him.*

NADIA Be clear: if what people are saying is that it's our duty to
  try and understand things from the other point of view, if
  they're saying we've all got to work out what the hell this is all
  about, then—believe me—I'm with them. One hundred
  percent.
OLIVER But?

OLIVER *waits.* NADIA *doesn't want to spell it out. She sips her wine.*

DAVID HARE

OLIVER But?

NADIA But that doesn't mean forgetting what we believe in.
Does it? We believe in something. We stand for something too.
Don't we?

NADIA *is appealing directly to* OLIVER. PHILIP *shrugs.*

PHILIP I don't know. I really don't know. Maybe she just had a bad
back.

NADIA Maybe.

PHILIP The fact is, in America, it's true, I do all sorts of things
which aren't strictly medical.

OLIVER What sorts of things?

PHILIP More, well, what people want.

OLIVER What they want?

PHILIP It's not strict medical practice. It's not orthodox medicine.

OLIVER What are you saying?

PHILIP You have to understand: In the States they're really keen
about fitness.

OLIVER Fitness?

PHILIP You must know that. Fitness is seen as a vital component of
health. That's what my clinics offer.

OLIVER Clinics?

PHILIP Sure.

OLIVER I thought you had one. One clinic.

PHILIP I did. I did have one. Didn't I tell you?

NADIA Now Philip has three. He's doing really well.

NADIA *grins, provocative.* OLIVER *throws her an uncharitable look.*

PHILIP Anyway, there's a fine line between formal physiotherapy
and—I don't know—providing the client with a general sense of
well–being.

OLIVER What does that mean?

PHILIP I've just explained what it means.

OLIVER It's not strict medical practice, you say. It's not orthodox medicine. Well, then, what is it? What do you offer? Give me an example. Beyond physiotherapy?

PHILIP All right, I have various people on the staff.

OLIVER People? People of what kind?

PHILIP Therapists, osteopaths . . .

NADIA Personal trainers.

OLIVER Jesus Christ, what are you saying, do you send people out for a run?

PHILIP Dad . . .

OLIVER I'm asking. I'm asking a question.

PHILIP What's so special about running? What's so demeaning about running?

OLIVER Do you go running?

PHILIP No. Not personally. I don't go running. I employ people.

PHILIP *turns away, appealing to* NADIA.

PHILIP Didn't I warn you? Isn't this what I said?

NADIA It is, but I don't see why you need to take it so hard.

NADIA *grins, enjoying herself.*

OLIVER Well, I must say, if you want to know what I think . . .

PHILIP I can guess what you think.

OLIVER If you want my opinion, I've done a lot of interesting things with my patients, but I've never taken the fuckers out for a jog. I mean, are you serious?

PHILIP This is a mistake. I should never have raised the subject.

OLIVER I'm just saying, putting in all that effort, years of study, education, hard work, and at the end of it all, what are you doing? Handing out those ridiculous little bottles of water and lifting weights?

PHILIP *shakes his head, trying to keep steady.*

PHILIP Dad. Dad, you know as well as I do that there are cultural
   factors in medicine. You yourself used to teach me there is no
   such thing as pure medicine.
OLIVER No. But there is such a thing as charging two hundred
   and fifty bucks to take obese Americans for a spin in the park.
PHILIP Do you think that's what I do?
OLIVER And there's a word for it too.
PHILIP Jesus, do you really think that's what I get up to?
OLIVER I don't know what you get up to. I'm a doctor, I'm not a
   personal healer.
PHILIP Personal trainer, Dad. Personal *trainer*, not personal healer.

NADIA *smiles, having a good time.*

PHILIP Dad, I take on people. Ordinary people. You say, "Tell
   them the truth and stay with them to the end." How about
   "delay the end"? That's not ignoble, is it?
OLIVER No, it's not.
PHILIP That's not wrong?
OLIVER Certainly not.
PHILIP "Put off the end." Why not? Get fit, feel better, sort out
   your problems.
OLIVER "Sort out your problems"? God, don't say you talk to the
   bastards as well!
PHILIP Isn't it called preventative medicine, Dad, and wasn't it
   something we were all brought up to approve?
OLIVER Of course.
PHILIP So?

PHILIP *waits.*

PHILIP So?

Still, OLIVER *says nothing.*

PHILIP We work to stop getting you ill, rather than treating you
once you become ill. What's wrong with that? It's the future of
medicine, Dad. Or did nobody tell you? Word not reached you?
It's all a damned sight more useful than writing prescriptions for
a living.

OLIVER Don't worry, there's no need to worry about it.

PHILIP I shan't.

OLIVER There's no need to be defensive.

PHILIP I'm not defensive. I'm aggressive. You're living in the past.

OLIVER It's your business. And it's not as if I have such a high
opinion of doctors myself.

NADIA Why not? What's that based on?

OLIVER I've met a lot of them, remember?

OLIVER *smiles, convinced.*

OLIVER If you think you're cleverer than your doctor, you're
probably right. A degree in medicine is proof of not very much.
It's amazing how many people will feel twelve peaches in the
supermarket before choosing the one they want, yet they go to
the first doctor without a moment's thought. Nothing
depending on it, of course, except their life. "Sorry, Doctor, I
didn't want to bother you." I watch them come through my
door: the more modest the manner, the more deadly the disease.
Cancer in particular being statistically linked to a recent upturn
in personal fortune. "Oh, Doctor, I had been through a bad
time, but recently I was just beginning to feel better . . ." Wham!

NADIA What's that about?

OLIVER Who knows?

OLIVER *smiles, at ease.*

OLIVER They look at you all the time as if you could help.

NADIA Can't you?

OLIVER Not if they won't help themselves. The first instinct of a sick person is to suspend judgment. Their immediate impulse is very powerful: they want to put themselves in someone else's hands.

NADIA Is that a bad thing?

OLIVER When told you're seriously ill, the easiest reaction is to surrender to what you think is authority. When it comes down to it, people would rather gamble than calculate.

NADIA Well, it's an easy mistake to make, isn't it?

OLIVER It certainly is.

NADIA After all, doctors are always telling us that they know things which we don't.

PHILIP Aren't they just?

OLIVER The job is to tell the patients everything I can. Then it's up to them.

NADIA Have you always thought like that?

OLIVER I'm a GP, remember? Behind me the ranks of experts, waiting.

NADIA Did you never want to be an expert yourself?

OLIVER I was an expert. Long ago.

There's a silence. They expect him to go on.

NADIA What happened?

OLIVER *smiles. Then he reaches for the bottle.*

OLIVER I'm going to give everyone another glass of wine and then we're going to go to bed.

PHILIP I'm going to take Nadia up Shep Hill.

OLIVER Take her up.

PHILIP *waits a moment. Then he gets up, picking up some dishes as he goes.*

PHILIP I need a jumper.

PHILIP *puts a hand on Nadia's shoulder, then goes out.*

NADIA What a gorgeous evening.

OLIVER Isn't it?

NADIA What time is it?

OLIVER Gone twelve.

NADIA He worships you.

OLIVER I don't think so.

NADIA Underneath.

OLIVER Oh no, not even underneath.

NADIA All right, "worships" is the wrong word. But he wants to please you.

OLIVER Not at all. He wants to get me out of the way.

NADIA Are you sure?

OLIVER He wants to forget me.

OLIVER *looks, unsentimental.*

OLIVER Believe me, this is not a visit of reconciliation. It's a visit of farewell. Because I suspect, whatever happens, I shan't be seeing a lot of you.

NADIA *looks at him a moment.*

NADIA I'm beginning to see . . . I'm beginning to understand how marked Philip is by his upbringing. He still feels bad he didn't become a doctor.

OLIVER Do you think so? I'm not sure. He was going to Newcastle to read medicine, but he never took up his place. It was at a difficult time. In the family. He said he'd rather do something less ambitious but do it better. Fair enough. Far less gifted people than Philip saw bones.

NADIA When I met him, in fact, what I liked most was his self-assurance.

OLIVER Philip has wonderfully high self-confidence and very modest self-esteem. It's a combination you find in all the most winning people.

NADIA Did he inherit that?

OLIVER I think you can say: on the contrary. Or not from me, anyway. You might say I've suffered from the opposite. Excessive self-esteem and no self-confidence. Hence.

NADIA Hence? Hence what?

OLIVER Hence.

OLIVER *is thoughtful for a moment.*

OLIVER Philip looked after his mother after I left. He's hardwired. That's what he does best.

NADIA Hardwired for what?

OLIVER No disrespect, but I think you could say he's drawn to difficult women. They've been a constant in his life.

NADIA Until now, you mean?

The two of them are still. It's seductively quiet.

NADIA And you?

OLIVER Self-evidently, yes. I'm drawn to them too.

PHILIP *appears silently, tense, behind them. Does* OLIVER *know he's there?*

OLIVER You'll like Shep Hill. The view is extraordinary. By day, they say you can see eight counties. And by night, the panoply of the stars. Weather permitting.

OLIVER *gets up.*

OLIVER I'll clear up tomorrow. Leave it for now. If you hear me in

the night, don't worry. I like to read. I like to read outside. Good
night. Good night, son.

This last to PHILIP *as* OLIVER *acknowledges him on his way out. There's
a few moments' silence.*

NADIA Well?

PHILIP *doesn't answer.*

NADIA Is something wrong? Do you still want to go for the walk?
PHILIP Of course I want to go for the walk.
NADIA Well, then.

NADIA *waits.*

NADIA I don't understand. Why are you angry?
PHILIP Because it's an act. It's a mask. You do know that,
    don't you?
NADIA Does it matter?
PHILIP He's not who he claims to be.
NADIA You mean underneath?

NADIA *smiles at the phrase.*

PHILIP What's funny? Why do you say "underneath" like that?
NADIA Oh. One of my students—something—anyway, this
    student kept saying: People are different underneath.
PHILIP Your student's right.

NADIA *waits again.*

NADIA What's wrong, Philip?
PHILIP He sits there so fucking reasonable, as if he were the most

reasonable man in the world. He drove my mother nuts. Why do you think she was so unhappy? Anything in a skirt he fucks it. He's fucked every woman from here to Akaba.

PHILIP *turns toward her.*

PHILIP And he killed one as well. Oh, by accident, it was an accident. But he killed someone.
NADIA In the surgery?
PHILIP No. Not in the surgery.
NADIA Where, then?

PHILIP *looks away.*

NADIA I don't understand. What's up, Philip? This isn't like you.

Suddenly PHILIP *is passionate.*

PHILIP People aren't their views, you know. They aren't their opinions. They aren't just what they say. They aren't the stuff that comes out of their mouths!
NADIA I know that.
PHILIP Urbane! Civilized! It's a trick. Anyone can do that. It bears no relation to who he is. All that high-mindedness! All that principle! The love of literature!

PHILIP *shakes his head in contempt.*

PHILIP And apart from anything else—I know you won't believe it because it's unbelievable—but he's trying to seduce you.
NADIA Don't be ridiculous. You dope!
PHILIP He is. He wants to remove his son's girlfriend and take her to bed.
NADIA I don't think so, Philip. I don't think it's likely.

PHILIP That's what he does. That's the sort of thing he does. Throughout my childhood. He smuggled a French prostitute across the Channel in the boot of a car.

NADIA *can't help laughing.*

PHILIP You think it's funny?

NADIA I do think it's funny, yes. For God's sake. You've got to escape this stuff.

PHILIP Oh yes? Have you escaped this stuff?

NADIA I don't know. I'm searching for any recollection of my father putting hookers in the back of his car.

PHILIP *shakes his head.*

NADIA And we say trunk. In the States we say trunk.

PHILIP What about a man who fucks some woman in the living room while my mother's sleeping upstairs?

NADIA Did he do that?

PHILIP Is that funny? Is that charming?

NADIA *concedes.*

NADIA All right.

PHILIP Just look back.

NADIA At what?

PHILIP At the way the day has gone. Look at it! It began with him undermining. The subtle undermining. Even you must have noticed the way he set out to subvert you. How he doesn't approve of you going to see the president.

NADIA Oh, that.

NADIA *smiles to herself.*

PHILIP How you must have sold out. How you must be some kind of raging opportunist for supporting the war in Iraq. In your own interests, he implied. For reasons of personal ambition, he implied. No integrity, he implied. Well?

NADIA *has no answer.*

PHILIP Then calculated—I promise you—calculated, not spontaneous: the switch. Oh, suddenly he doesn't dislike you. Suddenly he makes you a meal and he thinks you're great. I've seen him do it so many times. So the woman thinks, Oh, he's changed toward me. That's interesting. What an interesting man! God, it's so pathetically obvious. It's Casanova, page one.

NADIA Why does it matter?

PHILIP It matters because it's wrong!

PHILIP *moves away in anger.*

PHILIP And it's disgusting. My whole childhood a trail of women fucked over and spat out while my mother sat alone . . .

There's a silence. NADIA *speaks quietly.*

NADIA And you don't think now's the time to start to get over it?

PHILIP Of course I do. I am over it, I got over it. It doesn't matter to me anymore. I'm just pointing it out.

NADIA Good.

PHILIP What does "good" mean?

NADIA What do you think it means?

NADIA *waits a moment, taking him seriously. She's calm.*

NADIA Where's your sense of humor? Don't say you've lost it.

PHILIP I haven't lost it. I've mislaid it. I'll find it again.

NADIA When? When will you find it?

PHILIP Soon. I'll find it soon.

NADIA *smiles.*

NADIA Philip, we came for a vacation. We came as a couple. I
   want us to leave as a couple.
PHILIP Yes, well, that would be the definition of a successful
   weekend.
NADIA I've been honest with you. I've had a series of pretty
   unsettling affairs because I was always with untrustworthy men. I
   told you that. I can trust you. That's what drew me to you. Let's
   say, after some of my experiences, it was a very attractive quality.
PHILIP Was?
NADIA Is. It is a very attractive quality.

There's a moment's silence. PHILIP *speaks without bitterness.*

PHILIP Too difficult for you? Too much trouble for you? This
   whole thing too much trouble for the veteran of Sarajevo?
NADIA Just, I don't like to see people suffer over things they can
   do nothing about.
PHILIP I thought those were the things in life we *have* to suffer about.
NADIA I don't think so. No. I really don't think so.

PHILIP *smiles, conceding.*

NADIA So. Tell me. What are we going to do on that hill?
PHILIP What would you like to do on that hill?
NADIA Good.

The argument is resolved. They look at each other lovingly.

NADIA Let's both forget him. Let's leave him behind and walk up
   the hill.

DAVID HARE

ACT TWO

SCENE 1

PHILIP, *alone.*

PHILIP Asleep. Fast asleep. And dreaming of childhood. My father, the famous surgeon. The memory of my mother, sitting on the side of the bed, her hair tumbling over her face. Me, alone in my room, looking up at the sound of her crying, as if the plane to America were already waiting, one day, many years later, to take me away . . .

SCENE 2

The middle of the night. The lawn. OLIVER *is sitting in a dressing gown on one of the canvas chairs, reading, a small battery-powered light attached to the book. He does not hear as* NADIA *comes, sleepy, barefoot, from the direction of the house. She approaches, and he turns.*

OLIVER Do you know what Richard Nixon said when they took him to the Great Wall of China?
NADIA No. No, what did Nixon say?
OLIVER He said, "This is a great wall."

NADIA *smiles.*

OLIVER It's awesome, isn't it?
NADIA Kind of.

OLIVER What I admire: it's majestic in its simplicity. Of all the reactions a human being could have on being shown a wall, Nixon's is the purest. The most undeniable.

NADIA Nobody fools Richard Nixon.

OLIVER Quite.

NADIA He knows a great wall when he sees one.

OLIVER I think it may just be the all-time Zen remark of politics.

NADIA Did you just read that?

OLIVER Uh-huh.

NADIA Go get 'em, Dick.

NADIA *moves forward to look at the stars.*

NADIA What a night! My God, what a night!

OLIVER It's beautiful here, isn't it?

NADIA It's very beautiful.

OLIVER Aren't I lucky?

OLIVER *smiles to himself.*

OLIVER I don't think my son will be very happy to wake and find you gone.

NADIA He won't wake up. He sleeps like a log.

OLIVER Not you?

NADIA *doesn't answer.*

OLIVER How can you teach politics?

NADIA What?

OLIVER "This is a great wall."

NADIA Oh.

OLIVER Politicians don't speak words, they use them. How can you take people seriously who use language as an instrument?

NADIA Language *is* an instrument. Besides, politics is my life.

OLIVER Really? Your life is work? No other life but work?

NADIA *doesn't answer.*

NADIA Did you cook the supper yourself?
OLIVER Who else?
NADIA Single-handed?
OLIVER Did you think I brought it in?
NADIA How did you do the salad? It was delicious.
OLIVER Because it's a trick. It's a cheap trick.

NADIA *is looking out at the night.* OLIVER *puts his book aside.*

OLIVER Politicians only speak to please. Or to preempt an
    argument. Or to fill an uncomfortable silence. "This is a great
    wall." How can you teach that?
NADIA I'm interested in the art of settling differences. To me,
    that's what it's about. How do we all get along when we want
    different things?
OLIVER Is that what it's about?
NADIA I think it is.
OLIVER Nothing nobler than that? Nothing more heroic?
NADIA There are twice as many people in the world as there were
    twenty years ago. As more people live closer, their differences
    become more intense. For the Vietnam peace talks, two months
    were spent simply deciding the arrangement of the table. The
    war in Yugoslavia was resolved in the Bob Hope Conference
    Center in Dayton, Ohio. The session lasted twenty days. But at
    the end of it, there was peace. The good people are the
    negotiators. The bad people are the posturers. People say a little
    dissimulation, a little deceit is essential to negotiation. Well,
    maybe it is. But only so long as the other side doesn't feel
    aggrieved. Isn't given reason to feel aggrieved.
OLIVER Is that the secret? Is that the secret of how to succeed?

NADIA *looks at him a moment. Then she shrugs.*

NADIA Many of us, after all, came from Europe . . .

OLIVER Your own family?

NADIA My great-grandparents.

OLIVER Where to?

NADIA Northern California.

OLIVER Ah.

NADIA I come from a liberal background.

OLIVER I guessed.

NADIA Like your own, I assume. The way you think, the way you speak, they're familiar to me. The belief in public service. Public ethics.

OLIVER Are your parents still alive?

NADIA Why, yes.

OLIVER Together?

NADIA *shakes her head.*

NADIA Anyway—whatever—our first instinct as immigrants was to remove ourselves from your disputatious continent.

OLIVER Fair enough.

NADIA That's why we went.

OLIVER You were right.

NADIA To get away.

OLIVER Who can blame you?

NADIA And if you look at recent American history—World War II, Korea, Vietnam, the Cold War—then it's hardly surprising, is it? that so many of us are happier within our own borders? What's the point of being rich if you can't enjoy your wealth? When the Soviet Union collapsed, there was to be a dividend. We would live by ourselves and think about our own lives. But the opposite has happened. We're more and more drawn into the world. Do you wonder so many Americans are in such a bad temper?

OLIVER *smiles.*

OLIVER You weren't exactly drawn into it, were you?
NADIA Well . . .
OLIVER More like, you stepped into it, don't you think?
NADIA Depends which part.
OLIVER Barged in, I'd say. The West's been using Islam as a useful
enemy for as long as anyone can remember. "Shall we go to
Constantinople, and take the Turk by the beard? Shall we not?"
It's from *Henry V*.

There is a silence. OLIVER *speaks quietly.*

OLIVER Your feet will get wet. The dew comes early.

OLIVER*'s tone is so private that* NADIA *turns.*

NADIA And you? You read all night?
OLIVER I don't need much sleep. It's a doctor's trick. Snatching
sleep on the wards.
NADIA Everything's a trick to you. You use that word all the time.
OLIVER Do I?
NADIA Yes.
OLIVER I've watched the dawn come up so many times

NADIA *stands, not moving.*

OLIVER How was the hill?
NADIA I'm sorry?
OLIVER Didn't you go up Shep Hill?
NADIA Oh yes. It was spectacular.
OLIVER What did you do up there?

NADIA *hesitates for only a second.*

OLIVER I'm sorry. What a stupid question.

NADIA And the view was great.

OLIVER It is. It always is.

There's a moment's silence.

NADIA Philip . . . Philip began to tell me about his mother.

OLIVER Did he?

NADIA He began to open up. He talks very little about her.

OLIVER Maybe there's a reason.

NADIA *catches his tone.*

NADIA It was a bad separation?

OLIVER You could say.

NADIA He said agonizing.

OLIVER It was.

NADIA She lives in North London? In your old house?

OLIVER Yes.

NADIA She never left?

OLIVER *shakes his head.*

OLIVER Long before I decided to go, there were problems. She'd
    become obsessed with a need for control. To control life.

NADIA Her own life?

OLIVER Certainly. And, by extension, the lives of others.

NADIA She's a doctor too?

OLIVER *nods.*

NADIA What do you mean by "control"?

OLIVER It took different forms. It's one thing to put a label
    on the sugar jar saying "Sugar." You can put the word "Tea" on
    the jar where you keep the tea. But when you type the word

"Fridge" and put it on the fridge, then the signs are that you're in a certain amount of trouble. Easiest to say, her world shrank. From being a woman in the world she became a woman in flight from it. Even the trip to the hospital became unbearable to her.

NADIA Because?

OLIVER Oh, the feeling of being seen.

NADIA *waits.*

OLIVER The feeling of being watched.

NADIA Was she watched?

OLIVER Of course not. Nobody gave a damn.

NADIA Maybe that was the problem?

OLIVER I don't think so.

NADIA The feeling of being neglected. Your absences.

OLIVER *thinks a moment.*

OLIVER Look, you know, plainly it's clear—

NADIA All right, I shouldn't have said that—

OLIVER Say what you like.

NADIA No, it was wrong. I shouldn't have spoken.

OLIVER Philip has his own view of things, of course he docs. His mother's mental state is an issue between us. She's been on medication for a number of years. Philip thinks I'm to blame.

NADIA He didn't actually say that.

OLIVER Didn't he? It's no secret. Philip disapproved. Philip disapproved of our marriage. Of the kind of marriage we had.

NADIA What kind of marriage was that?

OLIVER The open kind. The kind in which love is free.

There is a silence. NADIA *says nothing.*

OLIVER Philip's also in flight.

NADIA Flight from what?

OLIVER Why, from me. Why did he go to live in America?

NADIA He's never said that.

OLIVER No, but you know Philip. It's obvious. Philip defined his life in opposition to mine. England. America. Many partners. One. Pleasure in discourse. Pleasure in silence. That's who he is. See it as a kind of strength. He's an interesting chap.

OLIVER shrugs slightly.

OLIVER For as long as he could, he tried to mediate between me and his mother. Then at a certain point he was forced to choose. I don't hold it against him. He likes me, but he'll never trust me. Who's to say he's wrong?

They look at each other for a moment, level.

NADIA Please. I'm not taking sides. I'm simply asking.

OLIVER It's fine.

NADIA There's no agenda, there's no motive. I wouldn't have raised the subject, but after all.

OLIVER After all?

NADIA We're alone on the lawn. There's no one around. And finally, I'd love to know who I'm sleeping with.

There is a guilty silence. NADIA backtracks.

NADIA Not that I don't. I mean . . . I don't mean that I don't know him. But I'd like to know more.

OLIVER smiles.

OLIVER It was you who said you needed private things to stay private.

NADIA I did.

OLIVER So? What is it? The night? The night is changing you?

There's a moment. NADIA *looks at him.*

NADIA In combat medicine, there's this moment, you know, you've probably heard of it—after a disaster, after a shooting—there's this moment, the vertical hour, when you can actually be of some use.

OLIVER Of use to me?

OLIVER *looks, disbelieving. Then he begins to speak decisively.*

OLIVER Very well. Our marriage. If you want to know. If you're interested.

NADIA I am.

OLIVER I've tried to understand. I've tried to understand what happened between us. But it isn't easy. How do you trace things back to the source? Pauline began to suffer from the very thing she most wanted.

NADIA What was that thing?

OLIVER Freedom. She suffered from freedom.

There's a moment. OLIVER *waits.*

OLIVER Pauline said to me, very early on, she said, I remember her saying, "I don't believe human beings need to practice holding on. Holding on is easy. It's letting go we need to learn."

NADIA Really?

OLIVER Yes.

NADIA That's a hard view.

OLIVER Is it?

NADIA Certainly.

OLIVER I don't think so.

NADIA It's a hard way to live.

OLIVER Excuse me, but I'm not sure anyone who makes their living as a foreign correspondent is in any position to judge.

NADIA Why not?

OLIVER What, rushing abroad to dangerous places?

NADIA It isn't that simple.

OLIVER Isn't it?

NADIA Are you telling me I'm running away?

OLIVER I didn't say that.

NADIA Well, what?

OLIVER All I'm saying: you didn't choose the most obvious way of life for someone who wants to invest everything in another human being.

NADIA Maybe, but I gave it up, remember?

OLIVER You said.

NADIA I got out.

OLIVER Yes, but you didn't give up for another human being, did you? You gave up, you said, because of your anger.

NADIA Well, it's true.

OLIVER That's why you gave up.

He waits. But NADIA *doesn't respond.*

OLIVER All right. So. Pauline arrived in my bed with no intention of staying there. We were carefree. We worked day and night.

NADIA You worked in a hospital?

OLIVER Yes.

NADIA That's when you were a specialist?

OLIVER Training. Training to be. Pauline was living in a certain way—we were medical students, we grew up in the sixties. For God's sake, the body's our field. If you've ever worried what a doctor is thinking when he asks you to take your clothes off, you needn't worry anymore. I can tell you the answer. Never underestimate the medical professional's capacity for filthy-mindedness. Pauline didn't plan to change just because she'd met me. You may not believe this, but people of that age, we had an idea. Underneath all the bullshit, all the evasion, all the "I'll see you tomorrow" when you mean *you won't—ever—*you'd cross the road if you so much as saw the other person coming—we actually had an idea.

DAVID HARE

NADIA What kind of idea?

OLIVER We believed.

NADIA What did you believe?

OLIVER Oh. The more people you sleep with, the more you learn.

There's a silence. OLIVER *is quiet.*

OLIVER The liberation of Eros. All right, it's no longer a
fashionable point of view.

NADIA You could say.

OLIVER But that's what we thought. We took it seriously. The
more widely you love, the wider your capacity for love becomes.

NADIA Did you really believe that?

OLIVER It was a different time.

NADIA It certainly was.

OLIVER Love's a feeling, isn't it? It's a feeling. It isn't the truth.

NADIA Is it?

There's a silence.

NADIA Go on.

OLIVER There was a lot of talk about ownership. About not being
owned. People not being property. William Blake to his wife: "If
you wish my happiness, how can you not wish me happy with
someone else?"

NADIA *grins.*

NADIA They're handy, these poets of yours, aren't they?

OLIVER Well, they are.

NADIA Never really on your own, are you?

OLIVER Not really.

NADIA You always have a poet around.

NADIA *shakes her head, disbelieving.*

NADIA I must say, it does take a particular gift, it takes a particular flair—you sleep with a lot of women and somehow you want to claim it *means* something?

OLIVER Well?

NADIA I have to ask, this "generation" you talk about—you think it was time well spent, do you, you spent your time well, did you, dreaming up a philosophy to justify what anyone else would have known was simple selfishness?

OLIVER I think it may go a little deeper than that.

NADIA Do you? What's the idea? You sleep with a lot of people and it's an *ideal*?

OLIVER Well, so it was.

NADIA I mean, the obvious question, why not just fuck 'em for fun?

OLIVER All right . . .

NADIA That's what the rest of us do.

There is a moment's silence.

NADIA Did do. Did do.

OLIVER Before you met Philip.

NADIA Quite.

NADIA *smiles, acknowledging the slip. She makes a gesture of "What can you do?"*

OLIVER You may be right. A failed experiment. Who can say? Though it didn't feel like that at the time. For a start, we were a lot happier than our parents.

NADIA Isn't everyone?

OLIVER *smiles, acknowledging the truth.*

OLIVER Or at least to begin with. Then, as time went by, there was a burden of guilt. After a while, the burden became intolerable.

NADIA Specifically?

OLIVER The ending of our relationship was, for one reason or another, spectacular. That alone. Has Philip never said?

NADIA *shakes her head.*

OLIVER But also the more general question: Could I have made this woman less unhappy?

NADIA Could you?

OLIVER How can you tell? I'm nearly sixty.

NADIA Does that make a difference?

OLIVER I've learnt a little respect for mystery.

OLIVER *smiles.*

OLIVER There you are. You become worn down.

NADIA I imagine.

OLIVER Strange thing, in the early days I was prone to gloominess myself. Pauline would say, "You know, Oliver, there's never been such a thing as a state-registered melancholic. You could be first to sign up." But when Pauline became so desperate, then my own moodiness no longer seemed profound. It seemed irrelevant.

OLIVER *shrugs.*

OLIVER The fashion now is to attack Freud. He's not acceptable, is he?

NADIA Freud?

OLIVER Not anymore.

NADIA I don't know. Isn't he?

OLIVER But there he is, working away, trying to define the impossible line between what we need to suffer and what we don't. We can try to understand each other, we have to, it's our life's work, but finally, Freud comes to us and reports that people remain unknowable. It's strange, isn't it? It's typical that we're all so keen to dismiss this man—"a prisoner of his time," we say— but in their resentment, their determination he should be irrelevant, nobody sees, nobody remembers: there's something beautiful about what Freud's telling us. So many scientists leave the world diminished. He leaves it enlarged. He doesn't explain life. Rather, he warns us to take care because so much is inexplicable.

OLIVER *smiles.*

NADIA Is that his message?
OLIVER Among others.
NADIA I've never really known.
OLIVER You don't approve?
NADIA Not that. More: one of my students . . .
OLIVER Yes?
NADIA . . . brought Freud up—only the other day.
OLIVER And?
NADIA And I did notice, it did occur to me, people usually talk about Freud when they want to get their own way. They talk about Freud because they don't like the look of the facts.
OLIVER You mean they use him because he's convenient?
NADIA Exactly. That's exactly what I mean.
OLIVER In what way?
NADIA "I don't fancy you." "Oh yes, you do. *Underneath.*"

They both smile.

NADIA Freud's used to justify everything, isn't he? "It's not my fault. It was my childhood." "It was my mother." "It's the way I was brought up." Hear the word "Freud" and it's like a flag. You know there's an excuse coming. I mean, wouldn't it be refreshing to restore the notion of *bad behavior*? And people being responsible for what they do? Wouldn't that be refreshing!

OLIVER Goodness.

NADIA I know.

OLIVER Well, goodness.

OLIVER *smiles.* NADIA *stands, slightly taken aback by her own outburst.*

OLIVER Something tells me you're winding up for a drink.

NADIA As a matter of fact, I am. Do you mind?

OLIVER Not in the slightest.

NADIA What time is it?

OLIVER Five.

NADIA Okay.

OLIVER Five's a good time for a Chardonnay.

NADIA *laughs and pours a huge slug from a remaining bottle.*

NADIA I'm sorry . . .

OLIVER No . . .

NADIA It's ridiculous.

OLIVER Not at all.

NADIA I know I sound harsh

OLIVER It doesn't bother me. Nothing bothers me.

NADIA But I travel in so many countries where all this stuff counts for nothing.

OLIVER I'm sure.

NADIA It counts for nothing! It means nothing!

NADIA *has raised her voice, vehement.* OLIVER *throws an anxious glance to the house.*

NADIA I don't know, you can't help noticing when you return . . . when I came back, last time, say, from Iraq . . .

OLIVER Is that when you met Philip?

NADIA Yes.

OLIVER How long ago?

NADIA A year. It was a year ago.

NADIA *stands a moment, thinking.*

NADIA What is it now? Seventy-seven journalists already dead, the most dangerous war in the history of my profession.

OLIVER Your ex-profession.

NADIA Okay. Anyway, this last time I went to observe, not to report. I went as an academic. Not that it matters. They kill you whoever you are. And yes, it's true, I came back to my nice job at Yale, I looked at these kids, looked at my colleagues, and I thought, I know I've got to resist this feeling, I know I've got to fight it, but these people seem spoiled. They seem soft and spoiled.

NADIA *thinks, then drinks her wine.*

OLIVER And so we are.

NADIA As if nothing worried them except their jobs and their bosses and their little love lives. And I remember thinking, I have no right to despise these people, I have no right to look down on them . . .

OLIVER Nor have you.

NADIA I remember thinking, I don't like this feeling, I don't like this feeling at all. I'm not different. I'm the same. Just as confused. Just as lost. Covering up by always having a purpose, always having an intention . . .

OLIVER But underneath?

NADIA Exactly.

There is a long silence. NADIA *shakes her head.*

NADIA "Underneath."

DAVID HARE

Suddenly NADIA's *eyes well up with tears. She stands, fighting them back. With no warning at all, she is crying.* OLIVER *makes the slightest move toward her, but she puts up a hand. Then she goes and pours herself a second large glass of wine.*

OLIVER So?

NADIA So—something I've never done—I went to the gym.

OLIVER Well, fair enough.

NADIA The classic response—go to the gym, make minute adjustments to the proportion of body fat to muscle, conform to the social norms. Skinny! Skinny! I was in the gym. I was standing there, thinking nothing, or rather just thinking, "Live a long life! Look as much like other people as possible!" And suddenly there was Philip. Standing near me. Incredibly composed. Strong.

OLIVER What did you think?

NADIA I thought, Here's someone who looks as if he knows who he is.

NADIA *shakes her head.*

NADIA Absurd.

OLIVER Why? Why absurd?

NADIA I suppose . . . I'm ashamed to say this. I'm not sixteen.

OLIVER It was romantic?

NADIA Kind of. Yes.

OLIVER Say it.

NADIA You're not supposed to like men's looks, are you? Aren't looks meant to be a sign of shallowness? They say, "He was good-looking, in a shallow sort of way." They never say, "He was good-looking and it was profound." They never say that.

NADIA *shrugs.*

NADIA Oh, be clear, it wasn't just his looks . . .

OLIVER Of course not.

NADIA For a start, I liked the idea that he didn't come from my world.

OLIVER Well, no.

NADIA He's not bothered by things that bother me. Nothing he couldn't do. Fix a car. My car broke down. Even my roof. He knew what shop to go to, he could retile a roof. There he was, within hours of our meeting.

OLIVER Up on your roof?

NADIA I remember thinking, I've never met a man like this. A man who can actually do things. I wanted him.

OLIVER looks at her thoughtfully.

NADIA I'd always associated passion with turbulence. With upset. This was passion, only benign. That's rare. That's very rare.

OLIVER I imagine, after what you'd been through, it came as a relief.

NADIA It did.

OLIVER I'm sure.

NADIA I might as well tell you, there are so many kinds of men who don't attract me. Include in that: journalists, academics, people who talk about politics all day.

OLIVER You mean people like you?

NADIA Exactly. I've never been attracted to anyone like me.

They both smile.

OLIVER So who does attract you?

NADIA Oh . . .

OLIVER You have the air of someone who's had their heart broken.

NADIA What makes you say that? Why did you say that?

OLIVER looks at her, not answering.

NADIA Out of the blue, out of the blue, you say that.

NADIA *looks shaken. She stands, waiting for him to explain.*

OLIVER All right. Last night, when you were talking, when you were talking about your past, I couldn't help thinking, This is a woman who's been badly hurt.

NADIA What, you think you can see right through me?

OLIVER No.

NADIA Though, of course, it's not surprising, is it, given your area of expertise? All your background, all your experience . . .

OLIVER All right . . .

NADIA All your women.

The mood has changed. NADIA *is on the attack.*

NADIA In fact, would you mind, can I just say something?

OLIVER Of course.

NADIA Earlier . . .

OLIVER Yes?

NADIA When you were telling me about your marriage? How difficult it was. How hard to understand. I found myself wondering—you were speaking so tenderly—with such longing—okay, it must be tempting—I've noticed the world's full of men telling you how wonderful their ex-wives are—but weren't you rather overdoing the clouds of romantic mystery?

OLIVER Was I?

NADIA It's one of those things. One of those gender things. Women's ears tend to get fine-tuned.

OLIVER Fine-tuned? Fine-tuned to what?

NADIA Lying. Men who lie.

NADIA *looks, unapologetic.*

NADIA You made a deal. Didn't you? Isn't that the truth? The two of you made a cynical deal.

OLIVER I don't think it is.

NADIA It suited you. As time went by, it turned out it didn't suit
her. She grew out of it. You didn't. Are things really any more
complicated than that?

For the first time she has reached OLIVER. NADIA *looks at him, then
almost laughs before she moves away. He speaks quietly, to himself.*

OLIVER I think they are. I don't think that begins to get near it.
NADIA In fact, I can't believe it, I sat here yesterday, I was sitting
here . . .
OLIVER So?
NADIA Eating my breakfast, you made me feel terrible, you gave
me shit about going to see my president . . .
OLIVER What shit? I don't remember giving you shit.
NADIA As if you could judge me! As if somehow you were
entitled to judge me!

Again, NADIA *has raised her voice, newly confident of what she wants
to say.*

NADIA The funny thing is, I didn't even mind at the time.
OLIVER Didn't mind what?
NADIA My interrogation.
OLIVER Oh, come on! Interrogation!
NADIA I didn't even notice. At the time I just thought, Oh, this is
an Englishman. I've heard about this: this is the kind of guy who
sits on his lawn and thinks it's demeaning to get involved in
anything.
OLIVER Is that me? Is that meant to be a description of me?
NADIA Charming as hell. But lethal.

NADIA *nods.*

NADIA But then I woke up . . .
OLIVER When was this?

NADIA Just an hour ago. I was lying there in bed. With a nut of resentment. I thought, I'm not cattle. I didn't come here to be examined.

NADIA *looks at him a moment.*

NADIA If you really want to know, I didn't go to the White House because I was under any illusions.
OLIVER Of course not.
NADIA I wasn't going for myself. I went because I thought it was necessary.
OLIVER Sure.
NADIA I went because I thought it might be useful. It might be worthwhile.
OLIVER I'm sure. I'm sure you did.

NADIA *waits.*

NADIA Well? What's wrong with that?
OLIVER I didn't say it was wrong.
NADIA What's the alternative? We just give up, do we?
OLIVER Of course not.
NADIA The rest of us give up?

OLIVER *says nothing.*

NADIA It's easy, isn't it? It's easy, your position?
OLIVER Do I have a position?
NADIA Stay home, sit on our hands, look superior, say this administration's nothing but a bunch of seedy alcoholics and crooks?
OLIVER Well, you could say that and you wouldn't be far wrong.
NADIA Yes, but like it or not, they're the party in power.
OLIVER Of course.
NADIA They're the guys.

OLIVER Of course.

NADIA And what do we do about the fact that on this one
occasion they happened to be right? Whoever they are. Fuck
their ideology, fuck their golf-cart morals and their tenth-rate
business deals—but I happen to agree with them on one basic
thing: it isn't a bad idea when people are suffering—when you're
faced with that scale of suffering, you act. You help.

NADIA *has raised her voice once more.* OLIVER *looks again to the house.*

OLIVER All right, no need to jump off a building.

NADIA I'm not.

OLIVER Defensive or what?

NADIA Oh, we're all defensive, aren't we? Don't we both have
things to be defensive about?

OLIVER *just looks at her, a little shaken.*

NADIA Yeah, sure, you're the generation that talked about ideals,
have I got that right?

OLIVER Roughly.

NADIA Everything had to be an ideal.

OLIVER So?

NADIA Everything was a matter of principle! You may have
noticed—we are more practical. What did I say to you? I admire
the practical people. We don't deck everything out in fancy
philosophy. We deal with what's there.

NADIA *nods, bitter, speaking from the heart.*

NADIA "Ancient hatreds," that's what they always tell you. In the
Balkans I got so tired of hearing that phrase: "Ancient hatreds."
Whenever people tried to explain what the hell was going on.
Oh yes, people love ancient hatreds, because if it's an ancient

DAVID HARE

hatred, what can you do? You don't have to do anything. They tell you all the time in Israel, in Palestine, in Bosnia, in Chechnya, in Ireland, "Oh, there's nothing you can do until these crazy people decide to stop killing each other. They *like* killing each other." Well, it's never true. What is true is that wherever there's a history of violence you can be sure to find unscrupulous politicians looking to exploit it. But underneath there are always rational causes. And "ancient hatreds" is just the phrase they drag out when they can't be bothered to do anything at all.

NADIA *looks at* OLIVER.

NADIA It's taken America years, you could say it's taken us centuries to understand that we have responsibilities. Everyone's been begging us, "Take your place in the world." Then the moment we take it, everyone starts screaming, "Oh no, but you're doing it wrong." Do you know how hard it was? Do you have any idea?

OLIVER I do.

NADIA This was an isolationist government! Suspicious of everything that wasn't grubbing for votes and making money. Do you think I haven't paid my price on campus? Kids with four-by-fours and private trust funds of a hundred thousand dollars a year, coming in Gucci jeans and designer T-shirts, saying, "Oh, it's a matter of principle. I won't take class with Nadia Blye."

OLIVER Has that really happened?

NADIA Nobody wanted to listen, nobody wanted to hear. I could have been in foxholes, I could have been shot at by every insurgent on earth—and kids would still come snarling up to me: "Hey, didn't you go to the White House? Aren't you the woman who spoke to George Bush?"

NADIA *impulsively moves away.*

NADIA What do you think? What do you think it was like? That
   day I went to Washington . . .

OLIVER I can't imagine.

NADIA It's true, I walked in that day, I thought, This is the oddest
   thing I've ever done in my life.

OLIVER I'm sure.

NADIA Who are these people? What am I doing here? And then
   you remember it's democracy you're there to defend. Yeah.
   Freedom. So. In fact, when it comes down to it, there's only one
   "principle." I'll tell you what that principle is: Roll up your
   sleeves, put away your personality, and get on with the work.

NADIA *is quieter now, her emotion raw.*

NADIA The only reason you're there, the reason you're talking to
   the president, is that you happen to be an expert on issues
   exactly like this. And isn't it better to talk to people we have
   nothing in common with? Isn't that better? Isn't that more useful
   than just talking to ourselves?

OLIVER Yes.

OLIVER *smiles.*

OLIVER Yes, by all means. It's better. Always assuming people are
   listening.

NADIA Of course.

OLIVER It's quite a large assumption. Isn't it?

NADIA *just looks at him. She is apprehensive now, nervous.*

OLIVER And you have to consider another possibility, don't you?

NADIA What's that? What other possibility?

OLIVER It must have occurred to you, I would have thought, don't
   you have to take care you're not being used?

NADIA *is quiet, no longer fighting him.*

NADIA Yes. Of course. I accept that. I know that. Of course I do.

OLIVER *shrugs slightly.*

OLIVER After all, I don't know what you told the president.
NADIA No, you don't.
OLIVER I wasn't there.
NADIA No, you weren't.
OLIVER I can only guess. I assume it wasn't you who said, "Do it regardless of whether it's legal." I assume you didn't say, "Drop bombs where you like. Don't take field hospitals, lawyers, sanitary engineers, doctors, or any of the apparatus that any decent resultant society might actually need. Forget those. Don't take enough troops. Just bomb and hope for the best." I can't see you saying that.

OLIVER *waits a moment. It is now very quiet.*

OLIVER I assume you didn't say, "Be sure to have no plan for civil society. Take no notice of international opinion. Manufacture intelligence from the most corrupt and dishonest elements in the country. Sanction torture. Ignore objections. Be deaf to criticism. Somehow, magically, order will come out of chaos."
NADIA No. You're right. I didn't say that.
OLIVER You didn't say, "It doesn't matter if tens of thousands of people get killed, just so long as they're not Americans . . ."

They both are still, NADIA *conceding at last.*

NADIA Jesus, what a mess.
OLIVER You could say.

NADIA We certainly made a mess of it, didn't we? Oh God, I'm so
    tired.

NADIA *is vulnerable. There are tears in her eyes again.*

NADIA It's so much easier to do nothing than something.

OLIVER *reaches out a hand. She takes it. There is a silence, he seated, she
standing, holding hands. Then, after a while,* NADIA *shakes her head and
goes and sits down at the abandoned dinner table.*

NADIA It's true. As you guessed.
OLIVER What's true?
NADIA I did have a relationship.

OLIVER *doesn't move.*

NADIA I did. A journalist. He's Polish. I'd been with him in the
    Balkans. Then, as luck would have it, who's the first person I
    meet when I drive into Baghdad? What you might call a hard-
    line reporter. Meaning: fair chance he's going to get killed.
    Meaning also: he doesn't give a fuck about anything. As it turns
    out, including himself.
OLIVER That's difficult.
NADIA It is. Or anyone else. Including me.

NADIA *thinks a moment.*

NADIA Six foot tall. Thin as a rake. Like a long, bony piece of
    string. A professional. Meaning: he has no opinions. Opinions
    are for idiots, he says. Oh, he gets angry. He gets involved. But
    it's the job he loves. Dodging bullets. He's unequivocal. He says
    he couldn't live in the West.
OLIVER What you're saying is, he's heroic.

DAVID HARE

NADIA Yes. Heroic. Completely oblivious of his own personal
safety. And in the evening . . . he likes to get drunk.
OLIVER What's his name?
NADIA Marek.

NADIA *looks away.*

NADIA I couldn't take it. He turned me inside out. Like gutting a
fish. I'd never known anything like it. I was jealous. Oh, not just
ordinary jealous. But wanting to be as alive as he was. So little
frightened. I thought, I can't do anything. I can't work, I can't
sleep. This will kill me.

NADIA *shakes her head slightly.*

NADIA Anyway, I came back to America. I met Philip. You'll think
me contemptible.
OLIVER No.
NADIA I want to tell you something. I shouldn't. You're going to
hate me for saying this.
OLIVER Please.
NADIA I thought, If I just live quietly with Philip, then I'll get my
private life out of the way.

OLIVER *sits back, as if this is what he's been waiting for.*

NADIA And that's what happened.
OLIVER I see.
NADIA It's been very peaceful. I've been at peace. I've got on with
my work.
OLIVER That's good.
NADIA The students don't bother me. The stuff on campus—it
doesn't touch me.
OLIVER Good.

NADIA Why should it? Philip's always there. He's there when you
   need him.
OLIVER Does he know?
NADIA Oh yes.
OLIVER About who came before him?
NADIA Certainly.
OLIVER He doesn't mind?

NADIA *doesn't answer.*

OLIVER What I'm asking: He can live with the difference?

NADIA *looks at* OLIVER *sharply.*

NADIA He's not second-best. If that's what you mean.
OLIVER I didn't mean that.
NADIA Good. He's different. Easier.
OLIVER And easier's better?

NADIA *hesitates.*

NADIA I thought so. Yes. I'd begun to think so. Until I came here.

PHILIP *appears silently behind them, in nightclothes. He is very quiet.*

PHILIP Here you are.
NADIA Yes. I was talking to your father.
PHILIP I can see. I was dreaming. I dreamt you weren't beside me.
   Then I woke up.
NADIA Philip . . .
PHILIP It's all right.
NADIA We were just talking.
PHILIP What else would you be doing? What time is it?
OLIVER It isn't yet six.

PHILIP *moves barefoot across the lawn, the two of them watching.*

PHILIP It's a beautiful morning.
OLIVER It is.
PHILIP Of course that's what you don't get in America.
OLIVER What's that?
PHILIP The softness. The softness of the dawn. Nadia's an early
  riser. So she's already at work when I wake. I look out the
  window for a moment. It's the only time of day when I do feel
  nostalgic.

There is a silence, no one daring to speak.

OLIVER Then what happens?
PHILIP Oh. I go to make coffee and I cheer up.

PHILIP *turns.*

PHILIP I'll make some now. Do we all want coffee?
OLIVER I'll make it. I can make it.

OLIVER*'s beeper sounds.*

NADIA What's that?
OLIVER It's probably a customer. I'm on deathwatch. A patient of
  mine. I may have to go anyway. Excuse me.

OLIVER *has got up, and he goes out, taking some dirty dishes with him.*

NADIA Well?

PHILIP *says nothing.*

NADIA Well?

PHILIP *still doesn't reply.*

NADIA Are you angry?
PHILIP Why should I be angry?
NADIA Then good.

There is another silence.

NADIA He hasn't said one single word in any way disloyal to you.
PHILIP Of course not. He's not stupid.
NADIA What does that mean?
PHILIP He has a strategy.

PHILIP *shakes his head slightly.*

PHILIP I knew you'd get up. I didn't need to look. I knew you'd go
to him.
NADIA Were you awake?

PHILIP *doesn't answer.*

NADIA And as it happens, I wasn't looking for him. It never occurred
to me. I simply had jet lag. I didn't even know he was outside.
PHILIP Didn't you?

There's a silence.

NADIA Talk to me, Philip. You use these silences. You use them
against me. Tell me what's wrong.

PHILIP *turns and looks at her.*

PHILIP He wants you to leave me. I know him. That's what he
wants. He wants to split us up.
NADIA Why would he want that?

PHILIP He's jealous.

NADIA Why is he jealous?

PHILIP Isn't it obvious?

NADIA Tell me.

PHILIP Because we have something he's never had.

There's a silence. PHILIP *looks at her and nods, as if knowing he's right.*

NADIA And?

PHILIP And what?

NADIA And even if that's true, why would I leave you?

PHILIP *doesn't answer.*

NADIA What possible reason would I have to leave you?

PHILIP *is quiet, regretful.*

PHILIP I had the idea we were perfectly aligned. When we met.
We both have the same way of looking at the world. What
you might call a basically helpful attitude. We'd die rather
than say so, but don't we both have this thing about trying to
help?

NADIA So?

PHILIP It's odd. You've traveled more than I have. You've
seen much more. But you still believe the world's all about
argument and reason. You're power-blind. It's funny. You
don't see power. It's like there's a dimension missing from
the way you see people behave. You trust their good
intentions.

NADIA Don't you?

PHILIP When I read what you write—someone does this, so
someone else does that. You simply don't see it, do you? You're
an innocent.

NADIA I'm not an innocent.

PHILIP *smiles, calm.*

PHILIP I was born to an unhappy couple, remember? So I see
  things differently. I woke up every morning, my parents were
  tearing each other apart. That's why I get along with everyone.
  That's what I'm good at. The conciliator. I've done it all my life.
NADIA Well?
PHILIP Until yesterday evening. I warned you against him. I said,
  Be careful. I told you to be careful. You deliberately ignored me.

OLIVER *returns with a tray.*

OLIVER It's a text message. We're losing her.
NADIA Who's that?
OLIVER A patient. It's all right, I don't have to go right away. She
  has a little time left.

PHILIP *is firm, a new resolution in his manner.*

PHILIP How much did you tell Nadia?
OLIVER Tell her?
PHILIP About your own past?

There is a silence. OLIVER *looks at his son mistrustfully.*

OLIVER Oh, I see.
PHILIP Yes.
OLIVER Some of it. A little.
PHILIP I've never told her about what happened.
OLIVER Clearly.
PHILIP I considered explaining to her on the way here. Then I
  thought, better she makes her own judgment.
OLIVER That was kind.
PHILIP I thought I'd prefer it that way. But it turns out I was
  wrong.

OLIVER *looks up at what* PHILIP *has just said.* NADIA *looks between them.*

NADIA Philip, what's going on? What's happening?
OLIVER Do you want me to tell her?
PHILIP I do.
OLIVER Why, surely.
PHILIP I'd like her to know.

PHILIP *waits.* OLIVER *shrugs slightly.*

OLIVER Of course. If it's what you want. After all, everyone
  speculates. I can feel it around me. I've lived here for years but
  people still whisper. It's funny. Sometimes I think I resolved to
  be a hermit but I woke up a pariah.
NADIA Is this about the person you killed?

There's another silence.

OLIVER Yes. That person. As it happens, it's what ended my
  marriage. It was an accident.
NADIA Well, I hadn't imagined you killed someone deliberately.
OLIVER No.

PHILIP *looks down.*

PHILIP Excuse me, I'll see to the coffee.
OLIVER Do that.

PHILIP *goes.* OLIVER *looks at her a moment.*

OLIVER Very well. You have to understand, I don't know if
  you know this, the guts are distributed between various
  specialists. I was a nephrologist. I was very much the man. The
  man you went to, in that ridiculous snobbish way people have.

"Who's best? Who's best for kidneys?" "Lucas for kidneys." I was very, very rich and conceited. Arrogant, in the way doctors are. I was always rushing, usually because I was in the wrong place.

OLIVER *stops a moment.*

NADIA So?

OLIVER Well, I told you, there were no rules in our marriage. On the other hand, things reached a point where I came home every evening to hours of reproach. So I generally made sure . . . it was generally easier if I wasn't late. I'd spent the day in the country. East Anglia. I was driving back.

NADIA Had you been drinking?

OLIVER No. I'd spent an afternoon in bed with a friend. I left about five. I thought if I can be home by supper, I can avoid the inevitable scene. I was on a country road. The man was alone. He was in his mid-eighties, in one of those, I never know what you call them, Trabants. Soft skins? Anyway, cars that aren't really cars. He went straight into me. He never even saw me. I'd signaled incorrectly.

OLIVER *looks straight at her.*

OLIVER The police afterward said it would have made no difference. It was what they call a fifty-fifty. Yes, I'd signaled left, intending to go right, but this man was on the wrong side of the road.

OLIVER *stops a moment, thoughtful.*

OLIVER You might say, all right, he was going to die anyway . . .

NADIA He was in his eighties.

OLIVER That's right. Sometimes at the hospital it used to occur to us we were slaving to save a human being who'd be dead in two years. But that's the contract. I've never lost faith with it.

NADIA What's the contract?

OLIVER Life at all costs.

OLIVER *looks at* NADIA, *apparently casual.*

OLIVER I also killed the woman.

NADIA What?

OLIVER Yes. She died at my side. In the crash. I was giving her a lift back to London.

There is a silence.

NADIA I see.

OLIVER She was killed instantly. We spun over and I laid her out in the road. Bad luck. She hit her head at an unlucky angle. Very little visible damage. She had a silk scarf round her neck. Soaked in blood. Very shocking. Apart from that, nothing.

NADIA Who was she?

OLIVER I'd met her at a party. You might say I didn't even know her. But of course I did know her. We'd spent several afternoons together. But I didn't . . . Oh God, it turned out she'd told me all sorts of lies. Almost nothing she'd told me was true. She was a fantasist. She was married. Something she'd omitted to mention. Not that I'd asked. That wasn't the nature of the venture. But still.

NADIA *is shocked, silent.*

NADIA My God.

OLIVER Exactly. From the bed to the roadside.

NADIA How old was she?

OLIVER Young. Younger than me. There was a husband, who was . . . impossible. Understandably. Wanted to sue me. A lot of stuff about the General Medical Council. But it was an accident. After all, in theory, I'd done nothing wrong.

OLIVER *is lost in thought.*

OLIVER It was Marx, I think, who said that shame is the only revolutionary emotion. And so. I gave her everything.
NADIA Pauline?
OLIVER I gave her the house and every penny I had.
NADIA You left your practice?
OLIVER I did.
NADIA And came here?
OLIVER I left London. I came to live in Shropshire. That's right.

PHILIP *returns unobserved, carrying a cafetière. He stops a little way off.*

OLIVER Of course for Pauline—for Philip also—it was a simple issue. My wife had always said I was a despicable person. So at last here was the proof. She detected the workings of justice. It was what I deserved.

OLIVER *smiles, mirthless.*

OLIVER For myself, I was tired of justifying myself to another human being. I walked out. I came here to be a GP. I didn't need to. But it felt clean, it felt refreshing to stand aside from the racket. I need enough money to live, to drink decent wine, to buy books. Why do I need money to put in the bank?

OLIVER *is quiet now.*

OLIVER To me, you see, the lesson was different. It wasn't what Philip believes. To me the lesson was: You need only one moment of inattention. Just one.
NADIA You moved away.

OLIVER Yes. To where I wouldn't do harm.

NADIA Do you still drive?

OLIVER Very slowly.

OLIVER *looks at her.*

OLIVER I see life for what it is: fragile. Every moment for what it is: potentially disastrous. And, at all times, I try to take care.

There a silence. OLIVER *has still not seen* PHILIP, *who speaks without moving.*

PHILIP Nadia, perhaps it would be a good idea to get going.

NADIA *and* OLIVER *turn, taken aback.*

NADIA I'm sorry?

PHILIP Earlier.

OLIVER Philip . . .

PHILIP As we're all up. Why not? I was thinking that way we'll get to see something we wouldn't otherwise see. The road to the Welsh coast is spectacular. Nadia should see it at its best.

PHILIP *is firm, standing, not moving.* NADIA *looks between them. Now dawn has broken and the sun's rays are falling across the table. Father and son stand looking at each other.*

NADIA Excuse me.

OLIVER Of course.

NADIA *goes out.*

OLIVER Philip. What is this? Explain to me.

PHILIP Why did you talk to her? Why did you have to talk to her, Dad?

OLIVER It was chance. I just happened to be sitting on the lawn.

PHILIP In the middle of the night?

OLIVER Yes. I was reading a book on linguistics. People are beginning to feel it may be the key to consciousness.

PHILIP And it's coincidence, is it?

OLIVER What's coincidence?

PHILIP That she just happens to get up from my bed?

OLIVER That. Yes. Coincidence.

PHILIP And you discussed me?

OLIVER Briefly. But not exclusively. We discussed others as well.

PHILIP *stands, still resentful.*

OLIVER Philip, I am not Lucifer.

PHILIP I didn't say you were.

OLIVER You can spend your whole life being angry with your father. It's a waste. Truly.

PHILIP *is listening now.*

OLIVER Who do you want to be thinking about on your deathbed?

PHILIP I don't want to be on my deathbed.

OLIVER No, well, nor do I. Nor does anyone.

PHILIP So?

OLIVER All right, I tell you, in the normal sequence of things, it's a bad sign if you lie on your deathbed thinking about your father! That is not a sign of a life well lived. I would say if you're still thinking about your father, you've got real problems.

PHILIP I won't be.

OLIVER Good.

PHILIP Don't flatter yourself. I won't!

There is a moment's silence. OLIVER *is quiet.*

OLIVER You ought to plan to be thinking of her.

DAVID HARE

PHILIP *looks, only half daring to trust him.*

OLIVER I mean it. She's worth it.

PHILIP All right.

OLIVER She's worth a whole lifetime.

PHILIP Really?

OLIVER Yes.

PHILIP You mean it? You really mean it?

OLIVER Come on, she's a great woman. You know that. She's extraordinary. However, you're going to find she has what Americans call issues. She has unresolved issues. And she has some incredibly stupid ideas. But there you are. You can't have everything.

PHILIP What sort of ideas?

OLIVER She thinks she can set her private life away to one side. In an admirable determination to get on with things which she regards as far more important. I've tried it. It's not going to work.

PHILIP You said that to her?

OLIVER Of course not.

PHILIP What did you talk about?

OLIVER Oh . . .

PHILIP Tell me.

OLIVER Nothing much.

PHILIP Tell me. Please. Dad.

OLIVER *looks at him a moment.*

OLIVER Your mother. Iraq. The woman I killed. Politics. Freedom. Love.

NADIA *returns, fully dressed, calm, humorous.*

NADIA All right. I agree. We drive toward nowhere.

OLIVER Very well.

THE VERTICAL HOUR   99

NADIA I'm happy. Let's do it. Let's spend the day kicking our heels and feeling remorse.

OLIVER Have some coffee first. Let me get the cups.

PHILIP Dad . . .

OLIVER Let me. I'd like to. At least have something before you set off.

He goes. NADIA *and* PHILIP *are left alone.*

NADIA I'm sorry.

PHILIP No. No, it's me who should be sorry. I don't know what happened. I thought he was trying to seduce you. I apologize. We can stay if you like.

NADIA *says nothing.*

PHILIP I feel foolish.

NADIA Don't.

NADIA *looks at him, then makes a decision.*

NADIA I think you're right. We should go.

They move together, and kiss. They stand holding on to each other. They look into each other's eyes. Then they part. Neither knows what to do. It's resolved, but it's not. Some moments go by.

NADIA Philip, I didn't mean to hurt you.

PHILIP You didn't hurt me. Really.

PHILIP *smiles.*

PHILIP We're all brought up to believe the most important thing in life is to be true to yourself. That's what my father believed. "I have to be true to myself." Well, it's bullshit. It's bullshit.

NADIA Why?

PHILIP What matters is how you behave to other people. That's what matters, Nadia. Isn't it? Isn't it?

PHILIP *waits for an answer, but before she can give one,* OLIVER *returns with a tray of cups and biscuits.*

OLIVER Here we are. Let's have the coffee. Then I have to go and watch someone die.

PHILIP Really? Do you have to? Why do you have to?

OLIVER Because I said I would.

NADIA Seems a good reason.

OLIVER The best.

OLIVER *fusses over the cups and saucers. A few moments go by, everyone struck by the strangeness of the situation.*

OLIVER Anyone take sugar?

NADIA *holds up her hand.* OLIVER *spoons some into her cup.*

OLIVER Philip, you always took milk.

They smile at one another. He hands them both coffee.

OLIVER Good. Excellent.

OLIVER *looks out at the hills.*

OLIVER What a splendid morning.

The three stand, nervously drinking their coffee.

NADIA We'll drive carefully.

OLIVER Please do.

SCENE 3

OLIVER, *alone.*

OLIVER I went down the hill. I sat at my patient's bedside all day. She was tougher than I'd thought. My beeper was going. But years ago I learnt: deal with one thing at a time. Do that one thing properly. She lost life sometime early that evening. I'd stayed with her to the end and I'd told her the truth.

SCENE 4

NADIA*'s office.* NADIA *is once more casually dressed. Opposite her is* TERRI SCHOLES, *an African-American, just twenty. She has not taken her jacket off.* NADIA *is holding an essay in her hand. She is passionate, disbelieving.*

NADIA All right. I don't know. I'm lost for a response. You're an intelligent student. You're more than that. You're an intelligent person. What are you actually saying? Is this what you think? Not: "I've got to do an essay, so I'd better write something." But: "I actually *believe* this."

TERRI *says nothing.*

NADIA Because, apart from anything, I think you and I have always got on—we've got on well, is that right? I don't need to spell it out, the first rule of any academic endeavor: it isn't enough to assert. Assertion is in and of itself valueless.

NADIA *holds the essay out, quoting.*

NADIA "Why did Bush go to war? Because he could." What kind of a statement is that?

TERRI *still says nothing.*

NADIA "Because he knew he'd get away with it." Do you call that a theory? "For Bush and those around him, the exercise of power was enough in itself. America went to war for no specific objective. Iraq was irrelevant to the war on terror and that was the reason it was chosen. The point of the action was its very arbitrariness. To demonstrate to any possible enemy of the U.S., however distant, however irrelevant, that no one should ever consider themselves safe."

NADIA *smiles and holds the pages out to* TERRI.

NADIA Yeah, well, it's an interesting thesis, but, unburdened by evidence, maybe it doesn't quite have the impact you hope.

NADIA *waits, but* TERRI *is not responding.*

NADIA I mean, Terri, I don't know, as a for instance, this is just a for instance, if you actually did want to prove such a thing—what would you say? Bush walked into the Oval Office and stuck a pin in a map? Oh yeah? *Did you see him?* This isn't a talk show. This isn't talk radio. It's not "Let's go into the studio and say stupid things." This is an essay. In a serious discipline. The causes and origins of the war in Iraq.

NADIA *shakes her head.*

NADIA Jesus, I hear this stuff—as you do. I don't know what's happened to my country. Suddenly everyone's a blowhard. Yale—I don't know how to put this—but the point of Yale University is—very simply—that it should be a blowhard-free zone.

NADIA *quickly corrects herself.*

NADIA By which—look, I'm not calling you a blowhard.

TERRI Thanks.

NADIA I understand there's such a thing as disaffection. I do. When you're young it's great to pretend that everything is meaningless. It's great. Why do students all have thick curtains? So they can sit in the dark and relish the gloom. But if I took this essay seriously, if I did you the honor of supposing you mean what you say, this is worse than gloomy. Unthinking force lashing out like an animal. The only message of politics—we are who we are, so get out of our way!

NADIA *looks at her again.*

NADIA In the nineteenth century there was a movement in Russia called nihilism. Have you heard of it?

TERRI Sure.

NADIA I think you have.

TERRI I've heard of it.

NADIA That's the irony. Of all my students, you're one of the few who would even know what it was. But truly, they should find you an application form. Do you remember what it was they believed in?

TERRI Nothing.

NADIA They believed in nothing! Exactly!

TERRI Random acts of violence.

NADIA Quite. That's what they believed in. Do you?

TERRI No, I don't. Not the violence.

NADIA Okay. Good. So just the believing in nothing. Terri, there's a darkness in this essay. There's a scary kind of hopelessness. Are you going to tell me what's going on?

There's a moment's silence.

TERRI All right. I'll tell you.

NADIA Thank you.

TERRI For a couple of weeks now, I've been breaking up with my
  boyfriend.
NADIA Say what?
TERRI My boyfriend's left me.
NADIA I see.

NADIA *frowns.*

NADIA Well, I'm sorry. I don't know what to say. I'm sorry.
TERRI Not as sorry as me.

They both smile.

NADIA No.
TERRI And losing him . . .
NADIA Yes?
TERRI Losing him . . . it's made me think hard. It's made me
  realize a whole heap of things.
NADIA About American foreign policy?
TERRI No. No, not about that. More about—more about, really,
  how I don't want to stay on at Yale.
NADIA Terri . . .
TERRI I don't want to. Not without him.

NADIA *looks in disbelief.*

NADIA Oh, come on . . .
TERRI No, I'm serious.
NADIA I know you are. That's why I'm indignant.
TERRI It's what I feel.
NADIA It may be what you feel.
TERRI It is. It is what I feel.
NADIA I can't believe someone as gifted as you—who fought as
  hard as you did to get here in the first place—is seriously
  thinking of quitting solely because of some boy.

TERRI He isn't some boy.

NADIA No.

TERRI He's not just some boy.

NADIA I'm sorry.

TERRI How would you like it if I talked about someone you
knew and called him "some boy"?

NADIA I shouldn't have said that. I apologize.

There's a silence.

TERRI I met him more or less the first day I got here.

NADIA And?

TERRI Just one example: every brick in this place reminds me of
him.

NADIA Yes. Yes. I see that. That must make it—

TERRI We've spent whole weeks by ourselves.

NADIA Sure.

TERRI Sometimes we'd close the door and days would go by.

TERRI *is a little teary, vulnerable.*

TERRI Okay, maybe it's part of the problem, I didn't bother to
make other friends. I didn't need to. And some of the people I
did meet didn't exactly make me want to meet any more.

NADIA No.

TERRI And also—I don't want to walk out on campus and see him
with somebody else. So, the point of all this: I put a lot of work
in that essay. It's serious. It may be the last thing I write.

NADIA *looks at her, thoughtful.*

NADIA No, it's just—look—I'm not your counselor . . .

TERRI No . . .

NADIA I'm your teacher.

TERRI It's fine. You can't hurt me. I've been hurt enough already.

NADIA All right.

NADIA *takes another nervous, speculative look.*

NADIA Just: I have some idea what you're going through.

TERRI You do?

NADIA By an interesting coincidence, this summer I broke up with someone as well.

TERRI Why?

NADIA Why? Well, we went on a ridiculous visit to Wales—or rather, the bit beside Wales—he and I had been pretty close, and yet for some reason, when I started talking with his father . . . I guess I began to see the son differently. You may think that's really unfair.

TERRI Well, it is unfair, isn't it?

NADIA I don't think so.

TERRI Was his father trying to put you off?

NADIA That's what my boyfriend believed.

TERRI That's what I'd believe.

NADIA Yeah. But I didn't feel that. I was only there briefly. But something was broken.

TERRI How do you mean?

NADIA I had this feeling—for as long as I stayed with Philip, I couldn't be true to myself.

TERRI *looks at her, unconvinced.*

TERRI Yeah, well, there's a difference, isn't there?

NADIA What difference?

TERRI You were with the wrong man.

NADIA I don't know.

TERRI And I was with the right one. It does make a difference.

NADIA Yes. Yes, it's just—reading your essay, which perhaps I now begin to understand, I have this uneasy feeling that you may have been doing what psychologists call "projecting" your unhappiness onto the subject at hand. We have to fight this, we have to fight our own feelings, we must try and be objective.

TERRI I think I am. I'm not that stupid.

NADIA I've never said you were stupid.

TERRI I know we're looking at two different things. First thing—my boyfriend has gone off with a girl who looks as if she eats shit with a dirty spoon, and also—second thing—I'm deeply despairing of the direction my government has recently been taking. I think I can hold both these things in my head at one time.

NADIA Yes, of course . . .

TERRI Without confusing them!

NADIA I'm not saying you're confusing them. All I'm saying is—*look!*

Both of them have raised their voices.

NADIA I suppose I feel this so passionately—it's terribly important you don't simply give up.

NADIA *picks the essay up again.*

NADIA You say here, "There is only one truth. The powerful exploit the powerless. Indiscriminately," you say. "And without any conscience. Rich countries are, by definition, massively self-interested and will never reach out to help anyone else. Whoever heard of a country," you ask, "which gave up power or wealth voluntarily? Nothing ever changes except by the use of counterforce. Reason never prevails."

NADIA *throws it down.*

NADIA I just ask: How can you write that?

TERRI Because I've just lived through the last five years. I read the papers. I watch television. It's what I've seen for myself.

NADIA You're twenty, Terri. What are you suggesting? Everything's cynicism, is it—already?

TERRI No. But why pretend? Why argue for things that aren't going to happen? Like the world getting any more sensible?

NADIA Because we have no other choice!

NADIA *has yelled out in anger, way beyond the demands of the situation. Realizing this, she moves across the room and speaks more quietly.*

NADIA This is what gets to me. Despair's an affectation. That's what I think. It's self-indulgence.

TERRI I don't think so. It's more like not fooling yourself.

NADIA *looks at her, then goes and sits down at her desk.*

NADIA I don't know. You must do what you think best. Please don't do it unthinkingly. All I'm saying is, just be careful. Delay any decision.

TERRI Well, I will.

NADIA In either context. Your studies or your private life. After all, he may even come back to you.

They both smile.

TERRI Thank you. Is that the end of the class?

NADIA I guess it is.

TERRI I'm going to give it twenty-four hours and then see how I feel.

NADIA Well, that's sensible. Good.

NADIA *holds out the discarded essay.*

NADIA Take this. I don't want it.

TERRI *takes it from her and heads for the door.* NADIA *clicks on her desk lamp to prepare to work. Then she looks up.*

NADIA Oh, and by the way, I should tell you, if you do decide to see out your time here at Yale, I'm afraid I won't be here to see it through with you.

TERRI Are you going to teach somewhere else?

NADIA Not exactly. No.

TERRI *waits.*

TERRI Are you going to tell me?

NADIA I don't mind telling you.

NADIA *looks at her a moment.*

NADIA I used to be a war correspondent. Recently I've noticed I miss it. I'm going back to Iraq.